D0453512

UNDER HIS WINGS

Other Books by
Dr. Hallesby

———

Why I Am a
Christian

———

Prayer

———

Conscience

———

The Christian Life

Under His Wings

BY

O. HALLESBY, Ph. D.

Professor in the Independent Theological Seminary
Oslo, Norway

TRANSLATED BY
CLARENCE J. CARLSEN, M.A.

PUBLISHED BY
AUGSBURG PUBLISHING HOUSE
MINNEAPOLIS, MINNESOTA

UNDER HIS WINGS

Copyright, 1932
Augsburg Publishing House

First Edition, November, 1932
Second Edition, December, 1932
Third Edition, January, 1933
Fourth Edition, March, 1933
Fifth Edition, November, 1933
Sixth Edition, March, 1934
Seventh Edition, October, 1934
Eighth Edition, March, 1937
Ninth Edition, December, 1937
Tenth Edition, June, 1938

Manufactured in the United States of America

Author's Preface

THERE are some Christians who are never troubled by difficulties of any kind. There is an atmosphere of matter-of-courseness, I might even say cocksureness, about their Christian life.

This book has perhaps very little to offer them.

It has been written for the many believing Christians who from time to time are filled with dismay at the Word of the Lord, and who almost continually feel weary and discouraged in their struggle against sin.

And it is my prayer to God that some of these fainting souls will find a bit of surcease, a brief period of respite, in the reading of this book. If it will also help someone here and there to *abide* under His wings, my purpose in writing this book will have been accomplished.

O. HALLESBY.

Publisher's Note

The popularity the writings of Dr. O. Hallesby enjoy also in this country may be ascribed to the fact that Hallesby, although known for his scholarship, is not standing on the platform lecturing on some theological question, but is walking by your side and just talking with you. His books are easy to read; the sentences are short; so are the paragraphs. The language is simple. He writes in a conversational style. He is sympathetic, direct, and helpful. He discusses vital subjects dealing with the Christian life. And the people listen to what he has to say to them.

The Rev. Clarence J. Carlsen, M.A., translator of "Why I Am a Christian" and "Prayer," has also translated the present volume.

AUGSBURG PUBLISHING HOUSE.

November, 1932.

Contents

Be Still Before the Lord

"Be still before the Lord, and wait patiently for him."—Psalm 37:7. (Marginal reading.)

THUS wrote the ancient bard of several thousand years ago. And the admonition is no less timely today. To be still before the Lord is faith's greatest and most difficult accomplishment. There are so many things which would disturb that holy stillness.

The world is ever restless.

But more so now than ever. Certainly there has never been in the history of the world such a noisy and restless generation as ours. The cry is: faster, faster,—on land and on sea, over the earth and under the waters!

The heart of man is ever restless.

But more so now than ever. It seems as though men fear stillness and solitude. They appear to have entered into a tacit agreement to help one another to avoid stillness.

We Christians, too, are deeply affected by the noisiness of our age.

One is tempted to ask if there has been at any time in these past nineteen centuries a generation of Christians as noisy and turbulent as ours.

There was a time when the people of God were called "the *quiet* in the land." But that was over 1900 years ago!

In the Scandinavian countries there was a time when the people of God were called "the readers," but I am not certain that the believing Christians of those countries rightly bear that name any longer.

To a generation feverishly occupied with external things comes the admonition: "Be still before the Lord." Is there any message that we need more than this?

He who dwells in the eternal stillness beholds our noisy distress and longs to be permitted to impart to us the eternal joy and power which come through stillness. He whispers therefore in a friendly way to all restless, exhausted, shallow, and spirit-forsaken Christians: "Be still. What you need is stillness."

The Lord was not in the wind, and not in the earthquake, and not in the fire; but in the still, small voice. And this voice cannot be heard unless one permits one's self to be drawn into quietude.

Seek stillness!

Seek the secret place of prayer. Seek to enter therein *oftener* than you have done.

And *remain* in the secret place of prayer until you become still before the Lord. If the bustle of the world and restlessness of soul follow you thither, then let the Lord examine you and point out to you what is wrong in your relationship toward Him.

For we should make careful note of this fact: If we cannot become still before the Lord, there is something wrong with us somewhere. There is some sin upon which we are unwilling to have the light of God focused. Or there is something in God's dealings with us in which we refuse to acquiesce.

Seek stillness while at work!

It awaits you. Even amidst the noisiest surroundings and during your most strenuous labors it is possible for you to live and move in the stillness of the eternal realm, before the face of the Lord.

Seek stillness as you walk down the street or the road.

Let quietude become your friend, your daily companion. Seek stillness while you rest. Then you really *will* rest and gain strength for body, mind, and spirit.

The greatest blessing connected with stillness is that we can hear eternity; we can hear the voice of the Eternal One as He speaks to our conscience. *Sin* becomes a living reality; it begins to loom large before our eyes and to weigh us down.

What grace thus to know sin! How it drives and draws our souls in their unendurable agony to the Great Physician!

In stillness we hear the message of the Eternal One to sinners; the message concerning the Son, the Substitute, the cross and the blood. We hear *God* as He speaks words of grace and mercy to our bleeding, trembling souls. And no one can mistake *that* voice after they have once heard it. It takes only a quiet word like that from Him to bring peace and assurance to our souls and to make us courageous and strong.

Be still before the Lord when adversity and suffering bring worry and anxiety upon you; when impatience, self-wilfulness, and fear of suffering arise within you. At such a time seek stillness before the face of the Lord.

Seek it often.

Remain long in solitude with God; it will bring stillness to your soul.

There you will hear wonderful things from the Lord. When He speaks to you about suffering, He will speak in such a way that you will never forget it. Henceforth you will look upon suffering in an entirely different light.

He who in stillness before the Lord learns obedience by the things he suffers, has won the greatest victory which man can win. Even of our Savior it is written that He was made perfect through the obedience which He thus learned.

Be still before the Lord when the joy of success attends you on every hand.

Seek stillness and acquire poise of soul by which to bear the praise, honor, respect, confidence, influence, and power which success brings you.

It is the daily prayer of my heart that the younger generation of Christians may be less given to outward things, may become a less noisy and vociferous generation of Christians, than the one to which we older folk belong.

May our young people see that the problem which confronts them today is not so much to expand our program of Christian work, or to increase the volume of our labors, or to speed up our work. Our problem is rather to develop and strengthen the *inner side* of the Christian life, to pray forth and to wrest forth a less strained, a more real and substantial, type of Christianity, one which will better stand the test of daily living.

Under the Blessing of God

"Speak unto Aaron and unto his sons, saying, On this wise ye shall bless the children of Israel: ye shall say unto them, the Lord bless thee, and keep thee: the Lord make his face to shine upon thee, and be gracious unto thee: the Lord lift up his countenance upon thee, and give thee peace. So shall they put my name upon the children of Israel, and I will bless them."

—Numbers 6:23-27.

THROUGH these verses we get a glimpse into the great privilege which was theirs who belonged to God's chosen people. Here the Lord ordains how the divine blessing was to be mediated to this weak little nation. When the people were assembled, Aaron, or one of his descendants—whichever one was high priest at the time—,was to stretch forth his hands and speak the above quoted words.

And the Lord promised to stand back of the words, saying, *"and I will bless them."*

When the Lord Himself wills to bless, neither men nor devils can hinder the blessing from reaching the one to whom it is sent.

We find in the Old Testament, especially in the Psalms, many touching expressions of how safe, how happy, and how grateful the pious Israelite felt because he was one of this people, and for that reason could live his whole life under the blessing of God. In joy and thanksgiving he would break forth into songs of praise, each song more beautiful than the other.

*

At that time there was only one people which could thus share in the blessing of God.

But through this one people the blessing was, in the fulness of time, to be made accessible to all nations.

This has now taken place.

The barriers of nationalism have been torn down. Christ broke down the middle wall of partition. He is now choosing unto Himself a people, the people of the New Covenant, from all nations, tribes, and peoples.

If God's chosen people of old was happy under the blessing of God, the new Israel is still richer and happier. The blessing which God in times past could shower upon His people was only preparatory, a symbol of the blessing which He so generously bestows upon the Israel of the New Covenant.

In the first place, we have a High Priest who is far more glorious than the high priest of old. With His own blood He has once for all made perfect atonement for the sins of His people, and won for us all the blessings of heaven. From His heavenly sanctuary He spreads out His pierced hands day and night over His people. From these hands the most glorious of all blessings drips down upon unworthy sinners: the blood of Jesus Christ, the Son of God, which cleanses from all sin.

What a joy to be a member of this chosen people, the people which has learned to take refuge under His blessed hands with body and soul, with their joys and with their sorrows!

Blessed are they who have learned to live *under* the blessing of God! Who have learned to live *by* the blessing of God!

To most people such words as these are merely empty phrases, such as they are accustomed to hearing in connection with religion, but to which they are heartily tired of listening.

To others, on the other hand, there is nothing on earth so real and precious, in fact, so indispensable, as to live their lives each day under the blessing of God.

When a man begins to become aware of the sins which he has committed during his lifetime and which he himself can never in all eternity undo, he is at a loss to know whither to flee. His sins pursue him, hound him, harass him.

It is then that he realizes his need of the nail-pierced hands and the atoning blood. In his distress he finally seeks refuge with the little flock which cannot live apart from the grace of God. With more fear than hope he tries to see if it is possible also for him to find refuge under the pierced hands, but is frightened away again and again. He feels almost as if it were criminal for him to dare to seek this haven.

For the closer he comes, the more clearly he sees his sins. The sins of the past are bad enough. But even worse is the fact that he continues to sin. In spite of his most earnest resolves he cannot desist from his former manner of living.

But not even this is the worst.

Still worse is the fact that he sins in desire, fantasy, and thought even more than he sins in word and deed.

Whither shall he turn?

He is defiled by sin without and within. Everything that he does, says, and thinks is sinful and unclean.

He has need of the pierced hands and the atoning blood!

But does he dare to come?

Can God receive sinners when they cannot desist from

their former manner of living? Can God forgive sinners
who feel that they have no remorse?

To such a person one thing has now become needful.

He is no longer concerned a great deal about what
others say and think of him. The one question upper-
most in his mind now is: "What will God do with me?"

No longer does he think of naming any terms upon
which he will come to Christ. He is willing to do anything, he will accede to every demand which God makes,
if he can only be saved.

This is what happens when a self-willed, self-satisfied,
and frivolous soul begins to feel the need of the pierced
hands and the atoning blood.

Let us also see how such a soul becomes saved.

This is the most difficult of all. He tries to repent,
to feel sorry for his sins, and to believe; but the one
seems as impossible for him as the other.

And in the midst of all this He is already saved.

For in the very moment that he in his distress turned
to the Lord and told Him the whole truth, Jesus spread
out His pierced hands over him. At that very instant
the atoning blood covered all his sins. And thus he
was saved, although he himself was not as yet aware of
it and therefore could not be glad because of it.

That is how much it means when our High Priest
spreads out His hands over sinners.

*

Godspeed to you, my dear reader, you who in your
spiritual distress confide in the Lord every time your
conscience makes you uneasy. You are already one of
that people over which the hands of Jesus are lifted up
unto blessing.

I know very well that it is not always easy for you at
first.

A little gleam of light now and then. A faint hope, which dawns upon your benighted soul. A passage of God's Word which affords you some help occasionally. A song or a hymn which suddenly banishes all pain from your soul.

But as a rule these things are but of short duration.

Whereupon it often seems to you that everything is in a fearful and hopeless state of confusion again. Doubts and fears assail you. You may even doubt God and His Word, but most of all you doubt yourself and your own experiences. You ask if the blessed moments which you have experienced and which you thought were from God were anything more than products of your own imagination.

All this is a part of your salvation.

But you do not understand it as yet; and that is why you keep on asking continually why the Lord deals with you as He does.

Nor can I explain all these things to you. All I can do is to tell you that that is how the Lord deals with all of us when He saves us.

All your doubts and all your fears, all your sighing and weeping, all your anxiety and distress cannot hinder the blessing from His pierced hands from dripping down upon you. You are already in the midst of heaven's blessings, even though you do not realize it.

This, too, you have in common with all of God's children.

Throughout our lives, even to our latest breath, we receive, because of Jesus' merits, a number of blessings which we do not understand and which we do not realize are blessings. But they come to us nevertheless, not because we understand them, and even less because we pray for them, but for the one and only reason that they are a fruit of Christ's death and are therefore sent to us by God without our prayer.

Permit me to bring this out a little more clearly.

You are not saved on the ground that you have repented, or have been sorry for your sins, or because of your faith. You are saved *for Christ's sake,* because He with His pierced hands imparts to you the fruit of His passion.

This He does, not because you beseech Him to do so, but because He loves you, and because He wills of His own accord to make you a partaker in the fruit of His death.

You on your part are asked to do only one thing: Confess your sins to Him. For it is written, "If we confess our sins, He is faithful and righteous to forgive us our sins, and to cleanse us from all unrighteousness" (1 John 1:9).

You who have confessed your sins and know that you have concealed nothing from Him, sit down and quietly thank Him because you are already under His pierced hands, because the Lord is gracious unto you, because, verily, His face shines upon you.

Praise Him because you are living by night and by day in the midst of that stream of blessing which flows silently but certainly from His pierced hands to all such unworthy sinners as do not by dishonesty and a guileful spirit shut themselves out from the fulness of this blessing.

✱

What a joy it is to belong to that people over which these pierced hands have been lifted up unto blessing!

Behold the believer's great advantage!

He is neither faultless nor sinless; but with all his failings and all his sins he is under the pierced hands.

That is what gives him boldness.

It makes him bold before *God*, even though he knows and feels that he is unholy and unclean without and within. He looks to the nail-pierced hands of the Savior and thanks Him because they cover all his uncleanness and because in Christ he has all that he needs in order to be well-pleasing unto God.

The pierced hands also give him boldness with respect to his own *conscience*.

His honest and sensitive soul feels accused and condemned all day long by the least little thing, as well as by the larger things. He feels that his heart is empty and dry, that he has no joy in the Lord, no sorrow over sin. His prayer life is stunted and largely a matter of habit, and the Word of God does not appeal to him.

Oh, how it annoys and plagues him—until he again raises his eyes to the pierced hands which are lifted up over him!

Then he realizes anew the meaning of such divine words as these: "Him that justifieth the ungodly . . ." And he gives thanks a little more humbly than before because he is loved in Christ Jesus as he is, and because he does not have to do anything whatsoever to win the favor of God. From day to day the nail-pierced hands of Jesus impart this merit to him as the free gift of God.

"The Lord be gracious unto thee!"

Thus the blessing was sounded forth in the Old Covenant. And in the New it resounds with even greater fulness, because grace has now been revealed in all its fulness. The message to every contrite sinner who now in all sincerity turns to the Lord is this: "My grace is sufficient unto thee."

With these words re-echoing in our hearts we can enter courageously upon the work and the struggles of life.

When the friends of Jesus weep and mourn over them-

selves, over their shortcomings, failures, and errors, then
the Lord draws nigh unto them and says gently:

"My discouraged friend, why are you so downcast?
Have you forgotten that I am God, that I am your Friend
and your Redeemer? My grace is *sufficient* unto thee."

Yea, verily, His grace is sufficient unto us. Every
day. Also our dying day.

*

"The Lord make His face to shine upon thee!"

This is a phase of the blessing which the Lord especially
desires to make known to us, not merely because we are
sorely in need of it, but also because this is the part of
the blessing which is most difficult for us to grasp.

When the Lord looks upon His people here on earth
below, despised by others and ashamed of themselves,
His holy face beams with joy at the thought of them.

He is glad whenever He sees one of His frail children
of earth. He is glad also when He sees *you*. Every time
His eyes run to and fro throughout the earth and He
sees you, He is made happy and His face shines.

And this He would have you know.

"Oh, no," you say, "He is not happy when He sees me.
My daily life is a source of constant grief to Him. I
offend and grieve Him every day."

I understand very well what you mean.

There are many believers who think: "If I could only
believe that God does not become weary of me, but continues to exercise forbearance toward me, I would be
more than thankful. That He should be pleased as He
looks upon me is absolutely unthinkable."

You are right.

We would never have thought or expected that such
was the case if it were not for the fact that the Lord
Himself has told us so.

That the face of the Lord shines with approval when He sees us appears unreasonable to us for the reason that we still persist in thinking that it is for *our* sakes, because we are so lovable, that God loves us.

On the contrary, it is for *Jesus'* sake.

What pleases the eye of God is to see a sinner who feels so poor and unworthy that he does not know what else to do but to take refuge with Christ, as the young of the mother-hen seek shelter under her wings.

Listen! The more helpless you are in your own strength and the more you cling to what Jesus has done for you, the more lovable you are in the eyes of your heavenly Father, the more His face shines when He sees you.

It is in Christ and not in yourself that you are well-pleasing unto God.

As long as you see that your sin and your uncleanness are so great that you must hide yourself in the wounds of Christ, so long does that same divine favor rest upon you as rested upon the Son: "Thou art my beloved Son in whom I am well pleased."

People who are parents can grasp this aspect of God's love more easily than others. But also they who do not have children have had experiences occasionally which throw light upon this mystery of love.

You were in the home of one of your friends. There you sat, engaged in delightful conversation. There on the floor was their child, rolling around, playing, or perhaps even crying.

Most likely you felt that the child was disturbing you.

But the father and the mother did not feel that way. Frequently during the conversation you noticed that they glanced over toward the little one with joy in their hearts. Every now and then they would look up from the little one and over at each other for a moment, and a beautiful smile would light up their countenances.

Why did the light shine out of their faces when they looked at the babe?

Because it was *their* child.

That was the whole secret. Only to *look* at the little one was enough to make them happy.

My dear child of God!

He who is the Father of all that is called father and all that is called mother and all that is called child in heaven and on earth, He feels for His children more than any earthly mother or father can feel.

You are *His* child.

He has *created* you. He has *redeemed* you. He has received you unto Himself in *holy baptism*. And if you are one of those who went away from Him, it was He who *called* you back and brought you to *repentance*.

Have you noticed that children are occupied principally, at least throughout most of their childhood years, with being loved of their fathers and mothers?

The principal thing that you and I should be occupied with during our brief pilgrimage here on earth is to let ourselves be loved of God, to let Him shower upon us His boundless love, to let Him in truth bestow His caresses upon us as His little children.

That is what He loves to do most of all.

And that is the thing that is of the greatest importance to us.

In the first place, nothing makes us so *happy* as to experience the love of God. It fills our souls with a quiet, peaceful joy, which transcends all knowledge and therefore all description.

In the second place, it makes us strong.

For "the joy of the Lord is your strength." Verily, temptations assail in vain the heart of him who knows that he is loved of God for Christ's sake. Never does sin become so repulsive as when the light of God's love falls upon it.

There is, therefore, no source of *sanctification as* rich as this.

＊ ＊

The Lord has created us not only with a soul, but also with a body.

And He has not forgotten that we are both soul and body. He blesses, therefore, not only our souls, but spreads out His blessed hands also over our temporal lives.

However, it is not easy for us to understand how God blesses us in this respect. Therefore, too, our temporal lives often become burdensome and difficult to us.

According to the Lord's plan, we should perform our earthly tasks in company with Him. It is His desire in a real, though invisible, manner to enter into everything we do and to add to it the *divine plus* which He calls His blessing.

He waits, therefore, for us to place *everything* that we do under His hands that He might bless it.

You who have *children* and are carrying a load of worry in connection with them and their future, leave your children under the blessing hands of God.

You know how exceedingly difficult it is to bring up children, in fact, you perhaps feel that this is the greatest responsibility you have in life. And you are right. But remember that God wills to enter into this work with you and add His blessing to everything you do for your children, both for their spiritual and temporal welfare.

It is the Lord's desire that you should do likewise with your *home.*

You have learned what a difficult art it is to build a Christian home, and you often feel very helpless indeed.

But do remember that the Lord will enter into this work also with you and add His divine plus to it.

Then you will experience what it means to have God send His blessing into your home day after day and make it the good, the beautiful, the peaceful place on earth that He intended the home to be.

The Lord will bless your *work* also, whether you do mental or physical labor, whether you work in a kitchen or in an office, in a schoolroom or in a factory.

Place your work day by day under the blessing hands of God, and you will see how the Lord will help you.

You will find that you will be able to do things which you at first thought were impossible of accomplishment.

How happy you and I would be in our work if we would thus learn to pray down God's blessing upon all our work, even upon the most insignificant part of it.

The Lord will bless your *finances* also.

This is a great problem to many in these days. Place this question also under the blessing hands of God. And do not grow weary in so doing even if you think now and then that you are not getting the help that you need and which you think you have a right to expect of your heavenly Father.

A few years ago I was studying in Germany. After having worked hard for some time I decided to take a little vacation during the summer; and with this in mind I took a trip to Switzerland in order to meet an old Christian patriarch by the name of Samuel Zeller, of whom I had heard and read.

Here I heard a story which I have not been able to forget.

It was after the Napoleonic wars, over a hundred years ago. Peoples and nations had been reduced to poverty then as now. Among many others there was also a poor widow. She had many children, and when she at last reached a point where she had no food left in the house, she was compelled to go out and ask kind-hearted people for help.

One day she went to the butcher.

He was not a kind man, and in order to soften his heart she spoke quietly and humbly:

"Would you please give me a piece of meat? We have no food in the house, and you know I have many children. God will bless you!"

At this a wicked smile stole across the butcher's face and he said, "Yes, you may have as much meat as this blessing of God you are speaking about weighs."

Then he took the smallest piece of meat he could find and put it on the scales.

But the scales did not move.

The butcher examined them to see if there was anything wrong; but no, the scales were in perfect order.

Well, he had promised the widow as much meat as God's blessing weighed; and so he put on another piece in order to make the weight go down. But no; it continued to remain stationary.

He put on more and more, and at last all the meat he had in the shop; but the weight stood still!

Do not you also think that God might desire now and then to show how much His blessing weighs?

Indeed, and not only that His *enemies* might see it, but also His *friends*.

Our lives would without doubt be different if we with the open eye of faith could see what God's blessing weighs.

What a bright and happy life would not you and I live if we could see that God quietly but assuredly supplies all our needs.

What peace of mind we would have while we were working if we went about our daily tasks with this assurance: "The Lord has given me this work to do, and I will do it *together with Him;* and He will bless the labor of my hands as much as He sees is profitable for me."

That would free the lives of Christian people from many things which now often tend to destroy their intimate fellowship with God and endanger God's cause.

That would put an end to all the little tricks and subterfuges which occur in the lives and in the conduct of so many Christians, because they do not believe that God's blessing is sufficient for them and theirs.

Christians who have learned to know what the blessing of God means have acquired *one* great and holy fear in their lives, the fear of so deporting themselves that the blessing of God must depart from them. They have learned to be careful at every point where there might be danger of doing anything which would hinder the blessing of God from following them.

They would rather suffer financial loss than to appropriate unto themselves anything which might seem advantageous but which would separate them from the blessing of God.

It is good to have such people to deal with both when we are buying and when we are selling.

God grant that our age might have more of *this kind* of Christianity, that the world might see in us and experience in all its dealings with us that we believe in the promises of God, and that we dare to act according to His Word.

When we begin to realize what the blessing of God means, the difficult problem connected with the giving of our means will also be solved.

In the first place it will give us courage to speak candidly with the Lord about the amount we should give

to the needy and to His kingdom's enterprises here on
earth.

In the next place, we will rid ourselves of some of
our natural fear of giving away money. A new, holy
fear will take its place, the fear of keeping money which
the Lord would have us give away. If we should keep it,
we would be cutting ourselves off from the blessing of
God.

*

I can imagine that some one will be saying to himself:

"I, too, have read what the Bible says about the quiet,
unseen blessing of God upon poor men's labors, and I
have seen it in life, in the lives of many Christians. But
I myself have never experienced it. I, too, have lived
with God and have prayed to Him, but no such blessing
has ever followed me."

And as you hear about this blessing again, you feel as
though the shadows in your life become darker than ever.

This is indeed strange.

I have met Christians who have struggled with economic difficulties all their lives. No matter what they
undertook to do, they were never *successful*.

They saw others prosper in certain lines. Whereupon
they, too, took up that line of work, but without success.

Then they tried something else, but failed in that also.
Thus they struggled along with financial difficulties all
their lives.

Perhaps such is the case with some reader of this book.

In that event, may I ask you to observe carefully what
the Bible says about the blessing of God: "The Lord bless
thee and *keep* thee!"

To be *kept,* then, is also a part of the blessing.

Believe it, there are many Christians who are praising
God for just this particular part of the blessing. For it

was this which enabled them to remain faithful to God and not sell their birthright.

Sit down quietly now and think of all the things from which God has kept you.

You are still clinging close to the Lord, even though it has been through many tears and many difficulties.

Many are they whom the Lord has delivered from the pitfalls of mammon by never having permitted their financial plans to materialize.

Many are they whom He has saved from the snares of vanity by having withheld from them both beauty and charm.

And many are they whom the Lord has kept from the lust of power and from the toils of partisanship by never having allowed them to acquire the influence they sought. They were kept down all the time. Thus they were prevented from growing away from the Lord.

Yes, indeed, as you reflect upon the bitter experiences of your life, all the difficulties you have had to go through, you see clearly by the light of the Spirit that it was all a *blessing.* You see that God was dealing kindly with you even in those days when, amidst sighs and tears, you were experiencing the blessing of God in the form of *keeping* grace.

*

But as you sit thinking of this, another thought comes to your mind:

"The fact that the Lord is compelled to deal with me in this way shows that I must be worse than other people. They succeed in getting through this earthly life without these great trials. But I suppose I have to have them because I am harder to bring up than the rest of God's children."

Now I do not know you, my friend, and therefore cannot say anything about you.

But I do know what the Word of God says about this, and I shall endeavor to point that out to you.

It is written, "For whom the Lord *loveth* he *chasteneth*, and scourgeth every son whom he *receiveth*" (Hebrews 12:6).

Scourging is a very painful form of punishment. Yet this is the illustration which the Lord uses when He desires to tell us what He does with those whom He receives.

And remember that the Lord does not exaggerate. He does not employ, as we do, strong language without meaning it.

When He scourges every son whom He receives, He fulfils what is expressed symbolically in the Old Testament about the furnishings of the tabernacle:

"Everything that may abide the fire, ye shall make to go through the fire . . . and all that abideth not the fire ye shall make to go through the water" (Numbers 31:23).

In the New Covenant these words receive their spiritual fulfilment in connection with God's bringing up of His children.

All who are able to abide the fire of suffering, the Lord makes to go through the fire; but all who cannot abide the fire of suffering, He graciously cleanses by making them to go through only warm water.

I believe that if we will look at this question from this side, suffering and tribulation will stand out in a new light to us.

We have just naturally thought that they who live on the sunny side of life are the happiest. But here comes the Word of God and tells us that the Lord deems otherwise in this matter. He does not think that those who escape suffering are especially fortunate.

When the time comes that we shall see everything in its

true light, then perhaps we shall also see that we were never accorded a higher privilege than to suffer.

This harmonizes also very well with what we believe about God. We believe in a *suffering* God, and we believe that the same God who suffers is also *blessed*.

My brother and sister, you who have been admitted into the school of suffering, you who have been cast into the fires of purification, and who feel the pain thereof both in soul and in body, do not become discouraged.

Above all, do not murmur against God!

I know you are tempted to do this when your suffering seems unendurable, but do not murmur. Rather pray God that you may be given grace to be still. For something great is taking place in your life.

God is working in your inner life and effecting your sanctification. He is purging away the dross in order that He may imprint His own image upon you, the quiet and lowly image of Him in His suffering, which cannot be impressed upon us except by suffering.

He Himself learned obedience by the things which He suffered.

Can we then very well expect to learn obedience in some easier way?

If you think at any time that your sufferings are too great, too heavy to bear, then turn your tear-filled eyes unto Jesus. Remember Him in His sufferings, and pray the Holy Spirit to reveal Christ unto you.

Pray, not only that you may *hold out* in your sufferings, but also that you may *see God* in them.

*

Most people flee away from the blessing of God.

His blessing meanwhile literally pursues them, because Christ has died for them too.

He Himself seeks them in order to bless them.

But they continue to flee away, farther and farther away from the blessing of God.

My fleeing friend, the fact that you are fleeing away from the blessing of God is the great *misfortune* of your life.

You think of many other things as constituting the great misfortune of your life.

And, of course, there are many things in life which are hard to bear.

But, nevertheless, your only *real* misfortune is that you are fleeing away from the blessing of God.

Remember that you are pushing forward along a pathway that the Lord has warned you not to pursue. Again and again He stands before you and says, "Not that way! Not that way!"

But you brush Him aside and continue in that very way.

Remember that you are going at your own risk as God calls to you and says, "I cannot go with you in that way. I will finally not be able to reach you if you persist in taking that road."

Why do you insist upon struggling in your own strength against the burdens, the hardships, and the sufferings of this earthly life, when God offers you His own counsel, help, and strength?

There are undoubtedly those who think:

"God has refused to bless me. From His heaven He looks down sternly and severely upon me and upon all my sins and failings."

Again you are mistaken!

Read the Bible and you will see how God deals with men: "He maketh his sun to rise on the evil and the good, and sendeth rain on the just and the unjust." He is One who gives us all that He can persuade us to accept.

We all accept the temporal blessings He sends us, such as sunshine and rain.

But when He sends us spiritual blessings, many speak up immediately and say, "No, no, no thank you!" . . . But they never get too many of His temporal blessings. We should, then, bear in mind the fact that God in His love gives gifts to these people even though He can not persuade them to accept anything but temporal blessings.

Here you see God!

He it is who grants you in superabundance the temporal blessings of life, and who waits for you to open your heart and receive into your life the greatest blessing He has to give us, Jesus Christ.

Have you never seen Him?

Indeed you have.

There have been times when the stillness of eternity descended also upon your restless soul. Then you, too, saw "the heavenly vision." Then you, too, heard the "music of heaven."

You saw Him whose hands were pierced.

You saw Him whose heart was pierced through because of the evil of our hearts.

You saw Him who allowed Himself to be tortured to death by His enemies in order to convert them into His friends.

Even now He stands by your side, meek and kind.

Flee from Him no longer! Listen to Him as He speaks to you!

Begin at once to read His holy Word.

And begin to pray to Him. Speak with Him every day about your sins, about everything of which your conscience accuses you.

It will lead you to faith and into vital fellowship with the unseen Christ.

The Holy Spirit will convince you of sin and lead you to the cross of Christ.

There your heart will begin to rejoice in the salvation which He has accomplished for you.

> O Jesus, Thou art pleading
>   In accents meek and low,
> "I died for you, my children
>   And will ye treat me so?"
> O Lord, with shame and sorrow
>   We open now the door;
> Dear Savior, enter, enter,
>   And leave us never more.

The Meek

"Blessed are the meek: for they shall inherit the earth."
— MATTHEW 5:5.

"Let your forbearance be known unto all men. The Lord is at hand."
— PHILIPPIANS 4:5.

THE word for meek in the Norwegian tongue signifies slow courage, calm courage, gentle and mild courage. These passages about meekness and forbearance thus speak to us also about *courage*. Texts which speak to us about courage are indeed timely ones. For we are cowardly. Every one of us. Some in one way and some in another, some to a greater and some to a lesser degree.

We are even more cowardly than others think we are. It is characteristic of cowardice to try to hide itself.

We are even more cowardly than we ourselves realize.

For we have very little courage even when it comes to being truthful. And therefore so little courage when it comes to facing and acknowledging our own cowardice.

Notice what happens when we have done something wrong!

Children are not alone about displaying great ingenuity in the direction of excusing themselves and wriggling out of the wrong they have done. We grown folk do likewise. Only we are more adept at devising excuses.

How seldom we meet men who without subterfuge of any kind admit their mistakes and wrong-doings!

We have very little courage when it comes to confessing that we have done wrong. Not only are we afraid of admitting it to others, but to ourselves as well. We are afraid that we will lose something by such admission, namely, the respect of others as well as our own self-respect.

That is why it is hard for us to ask forgiveness when we have wronged any one. To do so requires a great deal of *courage*.

Our lack of courage shows itself in all our relationships.

We have very little courage when it comes to *giving*.

We are not afraid when it comes to receiving, but we are when it comes to giving. That is why most of us calculate very carefully and reckon very closely when it comes to giving. Our sense of thrift is never more keen than then.

And we are not only reluctant about giving money. We are just as parsimonious when it comes to the giving of our time or our friendliness, our solicitude for others or our service. We do not have enough of the spirit of *sacrifice*. We quickly and carefully count the costs; and when we have considered them, we tend to shrink back in fear of the sacrifice involved.

We have very little courage also when it comes to being *humble* and unnoticed.

The desire to be great is deeply imbedded in all of us. And in few respects are we as laughable and as foolish as in this. We seek at all costs to avoid letting anyone see how small we can be. We even think that we have gained something when others get a wrong impression of us, and consider us better than we really are.

We have even less courage when it comes to *suffering*.

We are careful to go out of the way of suffering. God in His heaven likely never hears so many sincere and fervent prayers as when we beseech Him to keep us from sickness and sorrow, adversity and misfortune.

And it is likely that we never thank Him so heartily as when we thank Him for having spared us from sickness and trials of various kinds, while our neighbor is having a houseful of both.

Our courage, when it comes to suffering, is just as feeble whether it be a matter of illness, adversity, disappointment, or injustice.

It is perhaps most difficult for us to suffer *injustice*.

I know a number of people who have weathered storms of great physical pain and adversity very well, but who became bitter and hateful when they began to suffer injustice. It requires a great deal of courage to bear unfair treatment and injustice.

We see this even in the little things of daily life. If we in a discussion are certain that we are in the right, how difficult it is to let the other party have the last word.

*

When we finally see how cowardly we really are, it frequently happens that we experience an unusually strong desire in the other direction.

We even *take* courage unto ourselves.

Soon the desire also arises to *show* that we are men of courage. We wish to make it plain both to ourselves and others that we *can* think independently and act according to our own convictions.

We feel it unusually incumbent upon us to tell people the truth.

As a matter of fact, however, we do so more to show how courageous we are than how truthful.

Obviously, in such a state of mind it is hardly possible to speak the truth *in love*. On the contrary, we become harsh, cold, and unsympathetic in the truths we speak.

And if any one contradicts us, our state of mind soon reveals itself in contentiousness and imperiousness.

We are all reminded of how this can mar and oftentimes completely ruin a conversation or a discussion on Christian themes. We begin by keeping to the subject and speaking in such a way as to edify our listeners, but we often end in contentiousness and hair-splitting.

On my travels I have seen Christian men and women make use of the opportunity to testify of their Savior to their fellow passengers. Often it was a joy to hear how fervent and sincere their testimony was.

But what happened?

One of them would be opposed by somebody in the coach, and a discussion would be started, which would go along quietly and peaceably for a while, but which would at times end in violent debate. Their fear of being vanquished in debate would be greater than their zeal for souls.

Here was courage enough, but it was violent and unrestrained, without love and forbearance.

*

Jesus puts *meek courage* highest.

It is the *greatest* of all kinds of courage.

Jesus Himself had this courage and practised it all His life.

He had the courage to live unnoticed.

That He from early childhood felt and realized that He was different from others and thus had intimations of His high calling, seems clear from the account of His visit to the temple when He was twelve years old. And if He did have intimations that He was ordained by the Father to be the Savior of the world, it required great courage on His part to remain a manual laborer in one of the smallest cities of one of the smallest countries in the world all the while until He was thirty years of age.

He had the quiet, meek courage which dared to be as unnoticed as the Father for the time being willed that He should be.

That His courage in this respect was tested many a time during the long, monotonous years in Nazareth is very likely, even though the Gospels say nothing about it.

Already before His birth His mother had been told definitely by the angel what her Son was to be. She was therefore scarcely able to see Him go about His daily life like her other sons up to His thirtieth year without suggesting to Him that He enter prematurely upon His divine mission.

When the devil tempted Him in the wilderness it certainly was not the first time. At that time he tempted Him to intervene and perform miracles before the eyes of the people and show them who He was. The devil, no doubt, also tempted Him before that time to proceed to the exercise of His calling and not waste precious years. Moreover, the great temporal and spiritual needs of the people cried out to Him on every hand.

We find that meekness characterized the whole life of Jesus. Morever, He was true man, and "it behooved him in all things to be made like unto his brethren" (Hebrews 2:17).

Therefore He, too, knew what *fear* was.

And He did not hide this fact. In a fearful hour He exclaimed, "Now is my soul troubled; and what shall I say?" (John 12:27). In Gethsemane His anxiety of soul was even greater.

He never permitted Himself to be frightened out of doing what He knew was His Father's will. He had the courage to live His life according to the Father's will, to the exclusion of all else, unmoved alike by all well-meant counsel to the contrary, all cunning calculations, all satanic temptations, all the threats of those in authority.

The most courageous thing about Jesus was His *forbearance.*

"Who, when he was reviled, reviled not again; when he suffered threatened not; but committed himself to him that judgeth righteously" (1 Peter 2:23).

He was so certain of His right that He did not even want to make use of it, not to speak of demanding it. He left it to the Father to secure justice for His elect (Luke 18:7). His was a mild courage, completely under the sway of love; and therefore He could suffer injustice without being irritated or made angry by it.

He had the courage to tell the truth at all times, to friend and foe alike. He spoke it at times mildly, at times sternly, but always in love. For He never sought His own honor either when preaching or when engaged in a discussion.

*

This meek courage Jesus would impart to us.

"Learn of me; for I am meek and lowly in heart," He says (Matthew 11:29). Indeed it is into our *hearts* that this meek courage must be instilled; otherwise the whole thing will become a forced and unnatural imitation of Jesus.

Let us now see how He brings forth this humble courage within us.

He *begins* by giving us the courage to see our own cowardice, our own inherent fear of the truth.

In our spiritual awakening He gives us courage first to see how we have sought to evade the truth, how we have excused, bedecked, and defended our sins.

I wish to underline the fact that great, though lowly, courage has been brought forth in an awakened soul when that soul pauses in the light of the call of God as it falls upon his past life and into his wicked and unclean heart. It takes great and humble courage to give up all one's excuses and artifices and come forward and say, "I am guilty of all!"

And that is when it takes great and humble courage to remain standing before God.

Jesus alone can give us this courage.

A sinner who by the light of the Spirit has seen his sins would despair and never dare to turn to God unless Jesus gave him courage to do so. But by looking to Jesus, suffering and dying to save the lost, by hearing His gentle and tender invitation to come and receive full salvation without money and without price, the sinner receives courage to come.

We should also notice that a sinner will often hesitate a long time before accepting this gift. It seems entirely too great, and he does not dare to believe that it is for him.

There is a characteristic passage about the disciples: "They still disbelieved for joy" (Luke 24:41). Sincere, awakened souls must literally be compelled by Christ to accept the finished salvation which He offers them.

*

When an awakened soul has finally received such courage from Christ, then he has also received courage to be meek, courage to be lowly, courage to be humble.

He has learned of Jesus to be meek and lowly of heart. The mind of Christ is now in him, from which proceed all the meek words and actions of a believer.

Meekness thus springs forth from two sources, and by these it must constantly be fed if it is to continue to abide in the believer's heart and permeate his outward life.

In the first place, meekness characterizes the mind of the *humble* man, and proceeds from a sinful soul's real and sincere humiliation before God. If we will stand daily at the cross of Christ as doomed sinners, we will be more forbearing toward others, not only in thought and word, but also in our dealings with them.

The meekness which we reveal in our dealings with our fellow men is therefore a gauge which shows accurately how much we in our hearts have humbled ourselves before God.

In the second place, meekness never proceeds from humiliation and judgment alone. It is when a doomed sinner daily receives courage to accept *pardon* at the cross of Christ that he gains that quiet, humble courage which enables him to extend the same forbearing and sympathizing mercy toward his fellow men as he himself has received from God.

Meekness is therefore the mild and lowly courage of love.

The courage of *love* is the greatest courage of all.

What will not a mother dare for her child!

But, withal, a mother's courage is tender and mild, soft and gentle.

Let us hear what love has the courage to do:

"Love suffereth long and is kind; love envieth not; love vaunteth not itself, is not puffed up, does not behave itself unseemly, seeketh not its own, is not provoked, taketh not account of evil; rejoiceth not in unrighteousness, but rejoiceth with the truth; beareth all things, believeth all things, hopeth all things, endureth all things" (1 Cor. 13:4-7).

*

Meekness is not only the courage of *love;* it is also the courage of *faith.*

Faith and love are inseparably bound up in the life of the believer. This is manifest also in this connection. Meekness is a matter of faith just as much as it is of love.

We can without exaggeration say that to have faith in God is the most courageous thing in the world.

It is true that this sounds unreasonable, and it may seem as if it takes more courage to depend upon men than upon God. But we see every day that it is easier for men to depend upon other things than upon God.

That is why so *few* people repent and believe in God. That is also why those who do repent wait a long time before they heed the mighty call of God.

Søren Kierkegaard once said that to believe on God is like throwing oneself out upon a deep of 70,000 fathoms.

The courage to do this a sinner does not receive until God has made him aware of his sins and until they have become utterly unendurable to him. Not until then does he get that meek courage which is necessary in order to *will* to see one's self and one's sins in the light of truth, that meek courage which one must have before one will make an honest accounting before God. Then it is that one gets that deliberate courage which is willing to do anything except to be dishonest with God and himself.

But it is not only in the *beginning* that faith is an act of daring.

To have faith in God is a tremendous piece of daring *all the way,* even to our dying moment.

Jesus is the only one in the world who has dared to do this to the full. He is the only one who has trusted His heavenly Father so implicitly that He has dared to live His life wholly and completely in accordance with the Father's will and under His guidance.

We think that that involves too great a risk. And that is why we turn aside and follow our own ways whenever we think that it is too dangerous to obey the will of God.

In most instances we do not even stop to think that we are deviating from God's way, so accustomed are we to thinking that our own wills are wiser and better than God's will.

*

Let us consider this a little more in detail.

The Lord tells us that it is not dangerous to be lowly,

insignificant, and unnoticed. On the contrary: "If any man would be first, he shall be last of all, and servant of all" (Mark 9:35).

Think of the meekness it takes, the courage of faith, to follow this friendly admonition of His!

We all think that it is of paramount importance to be noticed, admired, talked about, praised. Even though we do not lay claim to genius, nevertheless we expect people to take notice of our talents, our ability, and all the other points in which we excel, both physically and mentally.

That is why we feel more or less disappointed and ignored if people do not appreciate our outstanding qualities and otherwise take cognizance of us. In fact, such disappointment is oftentimes so deep-seated that it destroys Christian fellowship and co-operation on a large scale.

In practically every Christian flock there is a greater or lesser number of both men and women who feel that they have been misunderstood and set aside by the leaders. They become peeved, begin to pout, and inject a great deal of bad blood into the group by slander and intrigue. Finally they surrender completely to the spirit of factionalism and divide the flock into two groups, thus doing irreparable damage for a long time to come.

Verily, it requires great and calm courage to remain unnoticed and to be set aside.

It requires the courage of faith.

A childlike and enduring faith in Him who said, "Whosoever shall humble himself shall be exalted" (Matthew 23:12). In Him who not only said this, but Himself lived according to it. In Him who was set aside, overlooked, misunderstood, and slandered; but who never did a thing to gain recognition from the leaders of His day or to become popular among the masses.

He did not only permit Himself to be set aside and despised.

He deliberately *chose* to be lowly.

For that reason He purposely avoided everything that would attract attention, knowing that it would result in a wrong attitude toward Him on the part of the people. With this in mind He performed a number of His greatest miracles away from the multitudes, and charged those who had been healed to tell no one what had happened. (Mark 7:33-36; 8:23-26).

It is not only in Christian circles that we are afraid of being unnoticed and set aside.

It characterizes all of our relationships.

Among friends and acquaintances alike it is the desire to make ourselves noticed which is responsible for many of our words and actions, more than we ourselves and even others think.

In our homes likewise.

We expect the other members of our household to notice us and to appreciate what we are and what we do for them. And if they do not, an element of dissatisfaction creeps into our hearts. In many a home this element becomes the cold fog which chokes out love and makes the home bleak and dreary.

"Let your forbearance be known unto all men," says the apostle.

The very first ones to whom it should be made known are those who are near and dear to us. They should be the first to reap the benefit and the joy which meekness on our part would bring them.

The home, too, is where we should *exercise* ourselves most in meekness, exercise ourselves in being lowly and unnoticed, and thus acquire courage to endure being set aside in the larger spheres of life.

*

Jesus advises us to *minister* unto others.

And He adds: It is not dangerous to minister to others. He knows, of course, that it requires a great deal of courage, a great deal of meekness, to serve others.

We are not at all opposed to being ministered to *by* others, but our instinct seems to tell us that there is a risk connected with ministering *to* others. We think we will somehow or other be losers by so doing.

We think, for instance, that we will lose *time* by doing others a favor. How many such favors have we not left undone simply because we thought we could not spare the time. First and foremost in our homes.

How these unused opportunities do cry out to us!

Especially when our dear ones are gone, and we can no longer do anything for them.

Verily, it requires the courage of great *faith* to take time to minister to others. For many of these favors are not always appreciated; some are not even noticed. Then especially are we tempted to cease ministering to others and to look to ourselves a little more.

We will without any doubt eventually cease ministering to others if we do not have faith in Him who seeth in secret and who rewardeth openly. In Him who Himself made use of His valuable time to go about and do good. In Him who on the last day will surprise us by telling us that to minister to others in a self-forgetting spirit is to Him the important thing in life (Matthew 25:34-40).

My dear reader!

You and I who are so occupied with our work and calling in life that we scarcely have time to do our fellow men a favor, should we not agree to ask God for that courage of faith which dares to take time to help others?

Even if we do not succeed in making a great and comprehensive contribution to life, and even if all that we do is rather scattered and disconnected, nevertheless, if we will only spend our lives and our time doing both large and small favors for our fellow men, what a great life-work we will leave behind us!

Looking at the life of Jesus, it seems clear to me that we can not spend our lives in a better way than serving others.

It takes a great deal of courage, a great deal of meekness, thus to spend one's life. I for one feel the desire to pray for that courage and that meekness.

We not only think that we lose time by serving others; we think also that we sacrifice our very well-being in life by so doing.

How many services have we not failed to render because we thought that we would be better off by not doing so. To serve others is a tax upon our own *comfort* and *ease*, and the latter as a rule mean more to us than we ourselves are willing to admit. When we are in the midst of our *work*, for instance, we find it inconvenient to be interrupted in order to do others a favor. If we are *resting* we find that such is even more the case.

As a rule, however, we are not honest enough with ourselves to admit that our love of ease is the real reason for not doing these things. Instead we devise "valid" reasons why we time and again leave people to serve themselves.

Verily, great courage and meekness are required to serve others, in particular to persevere in so doing. Only with the courage of *faith* can we succeed in doing this, faith in Him who said, "My meat is to do the will of him that sent me" (John 4:34).

If we will allow Him to impart to us this courage and meekness, then we, too, will experience a little of what He felt. It will become our meat, the satisfying of the deepest desire of our lives, to do things for others, for those who ask us as well as for those who do not.

Then we will experience the truth of Jesus' words, "Blessed are the meek." We can experience no purer and deeper joy than that which comes to us when ministering to others.

It is not only the people we have helped and the happy faces and appreciative looks we have seen which fill our lives with riches and joy. That which takes place within our own souls is even more important. To serve is love's most natural expression. That is why there is such joy and satisfaction in service, excelling all other joys.

Then even the most everyday sort of life quietly takes on a festive and holiday air.

Others are made happy, but we who have rendered the service are made more happy. Lived in this light, all of life becomes different. A common gratitude to God binds our hearts together. We get courage and strength to bear with one another even the greatest trials.

Jesus advises us to *give*.

And He adds: It is not dangerous to give. He knows, of course, that it takes great courage and meekness to give.

We think, as a rule, that to give things away involves a great risk. That is why we are so careful and figure so closely when deciding how much we are to give. All of a sudden we become great, expert economists, who know to the penny how many expenses we have, how great they are, and how much we have recently contributed to various causes.

At other times we do not as a rule exercise such strict economy, for instance, when we go into a store and buy something for ourselves or our dear ones. Then we are usually more liberal and do not figure quite so closely.

It certainly takes great courage of *faith* to give. By nature it is easy for us to look upon the money or possessions we give away as lost. Significantly enough,

we use the expression: to give *away*. Faith, however, has
the courage to give because it sees what unbelief never
can see: *the blessing connected with giving.*

First and foremost, there is the blessing connected
with having a part in relieving distress, helping those who
are in need, brightening the hearts and homes where
discouragement and despair have laid their blighting hand.

What a blessing it is to have a part in making people
happy and secure! Not only by the gifts we give them,
but even more by the solicitude and willingness to sacrifice which they thus meet, and which often restore to
oppressed and frightened souls that faith in mankind
which they have been on the point of losing. And if
they lose it, the world and life itself become a great
ice-house to them, in which their souls quietly freeze to
death.

In the next place, think of the blessing to ourselves,
the inward happiness and joy, which every voluntary gift
we give away leaves in our souls.

I am not here thinking only of the gratitude and love
which are showered back upon us by those we are privi-
leged to help, but of the very joy connected with giving,
even when our gift is slighted or even despised.

This joy is love's real joy.

Therefore it is in an absolute sense the joy of God.
His divine life from eternity and to eternity consists in
giving. That is His blessedness. He gives to the good
and to the evil, to the just and to the unjust, as Jesus
says in Matthew 5:45.

When we little by little give His mind its rightful place
in our lives and translate it into that love which *gives,* we
become partakers of divine joy, the purest and deepest
joy which God can give us.

If your Christian life is unhappy and empty, it is without question because you have forgotten to give.

Open your eyes and behold the distress which there is everywhere, and begin to relieve it by your sacrifices and your gifts. You will note a remarkable change, not only in your own heart, but also in your surroundings.

You will see everything in a different light: heaven and earth, man and beast, flowers and all. They will all smile to you, and you back to them.

Egoism *isolates* us, not only from men, but from all of life which surrounds us. Life closes itself automatically against the egoist. The egoist sees nothing but himself no matter where he turns, whether he looks at man or at nature.

Love which gives, on the other hand, is like a magic wand which opens the doors everywhere.

People who live such lives experience a wonderful and beautiful oneness with all of life, with mankind, the animal world, with plant life. We behold our fellow men and wish them well. We behold the animals and wish them well. We behold the plants and wish them well. We experience the deep joys and the quiet riches of life. We thank God for the unspeakable grace of just *living*.

We experience what Jesus has promised us: "Give and it shall be given unto you; good measure, pressed down, shaken together, running over, shall they give into your bosom. For with what measure ye mete it shall be measured to you again" (Luke 6:38).

Here we come in contact with still another blessing which comes from giving, namely, the purely material success which is the concomitant of the open heart and the open hand. God has ordained that he who gives shall not suffer want. He shall receive of God in return.

This sounds somewhat crass.

And many have taken offense at this passage. They say that Christianity encourages its adherents to speculate in generosity for the purpose of winning the favor of God and improving their own economic status.

But this way of thinking arises from a complete misunderstanding.

This misunderstanding would, however, soon be dissipated if men would actually try thus to speculate in generosity. It would soon be demonstrated that it is not the outward gift but the *spirit* in which the gift is given that Jesus looks to, today as well as when He sat at the temple treasury (Mark 12:41-44).

Jesus has Himself told us that he who gives in order to profit by his own generosity has already received his reward, and will receive nothing from God (Matthew 6:1-2).

He, on the other hand, who gives, prompted by *love,* to help others, and who therefore is not thinking of his own gain when he gives, him God will recompense. He will reward him not only secretly but openly, Jesus says (Matthew 6:3-4).

The fact is that he who gives with courageous faith in God and in love to his fellow men, experiences remarkable things in his own financial affairs. He finds that he always has a sufficiency of food, clothing, and money. He himself cannot understand how his scant means can suffice both for himself and his family. He gives to them who are poorer than he is himself, and yet he always has enough to supply his needs.

It is *the divine plus* which quietly and unnoticed is being added to everything he has and everything he does.

Everything is thus lifted up and placed on holy ground. He feels happy and secure at being permitted thus to be in co-partnership with the Almighty. He would not exchange with any millionaire who does not have the blessing of God upon his millions.

The meek have been given glorious promises.

"Blessed are the meek: for they shall inherit the earth."

"Learn of me; for I am meek and lowly in heart: and ye shall find rest unto your souls."

"God resisteth the proud, but giveth grace to the humble."

"He who humbleth himself shall be exalted."

*

1. *Rest.*

Love of honor makes us restless, weary, exhausted.

That is what makes the life of the man who is striving for honor a great tragedy.

He is always anxious lest he should not be recognized and noticed, lest he fail to make an impression, fail to succeed, and, above all, fail to forge ahead. This restlessness, of which he is more or less conscious, fills his soul at all times.

He who has the courage to be lowly and unnoticed is free from this gnawing anxiety. He experiences in truth the rest which Jesus has promised to the meek.

He finds rest in the fact that people do not overestimate him.

Usually that is what people do.

He knows this to be true because he has had the courage to look at himself in the light of truth. It has often pained him to think that men have over-rated him, and therefore expected too much of him.

He therefore experiences wonderful rest and joy when men do not overestimate him and he can be conscious of the fact for once that he really is more capable than people think.

He experiences the truth of Jesus' words that the meek are *blessed*. Paradoxically, he experiences joy in letting himself be humbled by men.

It is his fellowship with the Lord which is the source of this joy.

Never does he feel himself so united with Him as when he experiences humiliation. He takes up his little cross and walks willingly, safely, and joyously in the Master's footsteps, and experiences how his cross and Christ belong together, how taking up one's cross gives one's Christian life a joy and a strength to bear the burdens of life which one hitherto has never known.

At the same time it is a joy for him to submit all things to the judgment of God.

Whenever men misunderstand him and ignore him, he is driven anew into the presence of God. And when he has placed himself and his motives before God, he experiences a sense of security such as he has never experienced before, especially during the time when the recognition and favor of *men* almost hindered him from seeking the approval of *God* in all things.

*

2. *Grace.*

"God resisteth the proud, but giveth grace to the humble."

The sad thing about the proud man is that he by his attitude shuts himself off from the sources of divine grace.

The good fortune of the humble man is that he always maintains unbroken spiritual contact with the fulness of grace.

For that reason he possesses a wonderful capacity for living, both in his relation to God and to his fellow men.

His honest evaluation of himself keeps him ever in that state of spiritual poverty in which God can incessantly satisfy him with rich gifts (Luke 1:53). The Holy Spirit can each day explain the things of Christ to his troubled soul. He possesses quiet peace with God and a rich fulness of soul.

God gives grace to the humble, *in all of life's relationships*.

The very attitude of a humble man gives him a peculiar power to analyze clearly and calmly every situation in life.

He acquires a remarkable ability to associate with people. It seems that he can always approach them from the right angle. By his humility and lowliness of mind he succeeds in bringing out the best in all whom he meets. By his humility and willingness to serve he wins friends even among those who are opposed to him.

Everywhere he finds something to do for his Lord.

For he is faithful *in the little things,* and does not wait until he is given some great and outstanding thing to do. His is the meekness, the patient courage, which dares to leave the great things in the kingdom of God to others and himself do the little and unnoticed things, which only a very few have the courage to wear themselves out in doing.

Verily, God giveth grace to the humble!

Incalculable power emanates from these meek souls. Quietly and humbly they commend themselves to the consciences of all men. They are a sweet savor of Christ in every place.

Surely, no one is better qualified to win souls for Christ than the meek. They gain the trust and confidence of people wherever they go, and souls confidingly open themselves to them.

*

3. *He shall be exalted.*

"Whosoever humbleth himself shall be exalted."

God has promised to do that. And then we know that no man, nor any devil, can hinder it.

"The meek shall inherit the earth," that is, they shall hold the field of battle.

They have always given in to others, have always permitted themselves to be humiliated and ignored. Others have taken every right and every advantage, while the meek have never asserted themselves and never forced themselves ahead. In the bitter competition which there is between men they have always been among the vanquished.

But every time they were humbled by *men* they were exalted by *God*.

Now and then they also received *outward* exaltation and against their wills, so to speak, were raised up to high positions of trust, influence, and power.

I know Christian people who as a result of intrigue and partisanship on the part of others were completely misunderstood, slandered, defamed, and entirely ignored by the brethren. Moreover, they felt that it was out of the question to retaliate against the trouble makers; oftentimes it was not even possible to do so. By aggressiveness and arts and artifices of various kinds the defamers carried on until they finally dominated the whole situation.

The meek brethren involved were not only left out of everything; they were even stripped of their honor and trust.

But they had the courage to suffer humiliation and defeat. They looked to the Lord and committed their cause to Him who judgeth righteously. But it was a terrible time; it felt like being flayed alive.

But what happened?

After a few years of this the whole situation changed. The Lord exalted His humble servants. The wily machinations of intrigue were exposed. The real nature of their trouble-bent opponents was revealed, and the latter had accomplished their own undoing as far as the future was concerned. No one even thought of entrusting the leadership of Christian work to them any longer.

The meek brethren who had formerly been set aside were now not only vindicated before the eyes of all, but by the meekness with which they had conducted themselves while being persecuted they had won new and even greater confidence among the brethren, and thus been made better fitted than ever to be of service to the Christian people of the community.

True, it does not always turn out that way.

The Lord has His own ways, and does as He wills. His own Son had to endure humiliation and persecution even unto death. And by His death His enemies had seemingly triumphed.

In the same way, without question, He also deals with many of His children.

They receive no *outward* vindication. The Lord desires to exalt them in some other way. And when the Lord wills to exalt neither man nor devil can prevent Him.

He endows meek and patient souls with an *inner* spiritual exaltation, which commends itself to the consciences of men, a spiritual nobility which shines out from their beautiful souls and which imparts even to their outward beings something fine and glorious: a purity of soul and an unfeigned dignity which people cannot help but notice.

The fact that these souls are not themselves aware that they possess this inner exaltation only serves to make an even greater impression upon their fellow men.

It is with them as with Moses when he came down from the mountain after his meeting with the Lord: His face shone, but he himself did not know it.

"Let your forbearance be known unto all men."

This joy, too, the meek experience: Their forbearance becomes plainly evident to all men—except themselves.

Under His Wings

"He that dwelleth in the secret place of the Most High shall abide under the shadow of the Almighty. I will say of Jehovah, He is my refuge and my fortress; my God, in whom I trust."
—PSALM 91:1-2.

MY mother died when I was twelve years old. I have therefore only childhood recollections of her. But they are fresh and clear in my memory. Mother was sickly as far back as I can remember. She was not bed-ridden, but she did have to keep to her chair a great deal of the time.—Father had thoughtfully provided a comfortable chair for her.

I remember her best in that chair. There she would sit day after day in the living room, with her knitting or with a book.

We always knew where to find mother.

Especially do I remember the long winter evenings. Then we children played in the room where mother was sitting.

We had to be quiet, because mother could not stand noise. But how cozy and congenial it was as she sat there in our midst and helped us with our work and played with us, talking to us in her quiet voice and smiling her sweet smiles!

Merely the recollection of the security and well-being which I then felt does me good even today, forty-five to fifty years afterwards.

This childhood memory throws a light and sheds a glory all of its own upon this passage about "the secret place of the Most High" and "the shadow of the Almighty."

It teaches us how God would have us live the Christian life.

It should be the great privilege of our lives to live our brief span of years at the feet of the Almighty, in the secret place of the Most High.

In our homes, in the midst of our daily lives, is God, the great and good Father, with whom we are safe. It is His desire that we as His children should play in His presence, as well as do our work under His fatherly guidance, with His smile upon us.

The life which we are called upon to live is a difficult and a complex life, full of grief and pain.

The world in which we live is terrible: wicked, unsafe, dangerous. And, worst of all, it will never be otherwise as long as sin and sinners dwell therein.

Not even God can prevent this.

In a world of sin, sorrow, suffering, and death there is only *one place* where a troubled and aching soul can find release, peace, and security, and that is in the secret place of the Most High.

God Himself has no other means of helping sinners in this sinful world. But, on the other hand, the help which He does proffer is sufficient for all our needs.

I can still remember clearly that only to have mother near was enough to impart a peculiar sense of security to my childhood years.

In a far deeper sense is this true of God. Only to be in His presence affords the soul the refuge, the secret place, which it needs in its struggles against the evil and dangerous forces which seek to conquer it.

Mother's cozy living room at home could not dispel the wickedness of the world outside. But it could hinder its dangerous influence from reaching us. In that room we felt safe.

Within its walls we were clothed with that invisible armor which made it possible for us to go in and out in a wicked and dangerous world without being harmed.

In the secret place of the Most High, in the nearness of God, we gain that sense of security in life which every man needs in order to be delivered from the dread of life and the fear of death which hang like a suffocating pall over all of us, even though we are not always conscious of it.

They act as an undertow in the depths of our souls, and cast their shadows into our lives.

But our God is such that we need but be in His presence and a sense of security dawns upon us, just as surely as light follows the sun.

This is because God is God.

By being in God's nearness, then, we become rightly orientated with respect to all of life, including this wicked and dangerous world with all its misery.

From the secret place of the Most High we learn to look at everything around us in the right light, both men and devils, sorrows and joys, prosperity and adversity, suffering and death.

God's nearness does not alter the fact of sin, nor does it eliminate the dangers of life, the wickedness of the devil, sorrow or death. But God's nearness does impart a sense of security in the face of all that is evil and dangerous. In God's nearness I can don that secret armor with which I can walk with safety in the midst of danger and evil.

But we forget so easily this secret place which the Lord has prepared for our harassed and anxious souls.

There is an old song to the effect that our sins trouble us more than anything else, even in our happiest hours.

Our daily shortcomings make us restless and discouraged.

A conscientious Christian is conscious of the fact that he sins every day both against God and man, in thought, word, and deed.

Above all he sees his sins of omission, which more clearly than anything else show him how little he is living for others.

He sees the worldliness of his own mind, his slothfulness in prayer, his indifference toward the Word of God, his unfaithfulness and disobedience with respect to the promptings of the Spirit.

It more than pains him.

It makes him restless and uneasy. Often he is not certain whether he is a child of God or not, whether or not he has a Biblical right to lay hold of the gracious promises of God, and whether or not he is sinning against grace and practicing that spiritual guile which will forever exclude him from the salvation of God.

Then it becomes necessary to seek covert in the secret place of the Most High.

When a storm or a bird of prey approaches, the young of the mother hen hasten to take refuge under her wings.

In a similar way, let the storm of accusations which the adversary of your soul raises against you drive you into the secret place of the Most High. There everything has been made ready to receive just such as you. He awaits you, and grieves over the fact that you are not continually hiding yourself in His blessed wounds.

*

"But," you say, "is this possible?"

"I have misused the grace of God terribly in times past. Will I not again be taking the grace of God in vain?"

And your last state becomes worse than the first.

My friend, you forget what the Lord Himself has said

about this: "They that are in health have no need of a
physician; but they that are sick."

Those who come to Him do not come because they have
succeeded in eradicating all sinfulness from their lives
or because they have overcome the slothfulness and
worldliness of their hearts. They come because they have
not succeeded in this, because they cannot excuse or defend either their sins of commission or their sins of
omission, and because their lives have been made miserable by them.

Access to the secret place of the Most High is open
and free to all who *will*.

"He that will, let him take the water of life freely"
(Revelation 22:17).

"Him that cometh to me I will in no wise cast out"
(John 6:37).

"If we confess our sins, he is faithful and righteous
to forgive us our sins, and to cleanse us from all unrighteousness" (1 John 1:9).

"He that hath no money, come ye, buy, and eat; yea,
come, buy wine and milk without money and without
price" (Isaiah 55:1).

To the secret place of the Most High come all the poor
sinners of earth, with their sins and shortcomings of each
day and with their worldly, slothful, lukewarm, and
rebellious hearts. Everything they have done accuses
and condemns them. Nothing can abide the light of God.

Even the good that they do becomes stained by a dark
spot or two of selfishness or love of honor before it is
done.

And because they have chosen to allow themselves to
be convinced of sin by the Spirit of God they do not
attempt to shield themselves at all. Every arrow of truth
pierces to the very depths of their hearts.

There is one, and only one, place where they can find peace: In the secret place of the Most High, beneath the cross of Jesus. Only the blood of Christ can hide them from the divine wrath which is constantly proclaimed against them by the truthful and authoritative voice of their consciences.

At the cross of Christ we have a real place of refuge.

Whenever a believing soul humbles himself before the spirit of truth and permits himself to be convinced that "in me, that is, in my flesh, dwelleth no good thing," whenever he surrenders all thought of being anything in himself, then he quietly takes refuge in the pierced hands of Christ.

And the Savior whispers gently into his broken and contrite heart: "My grace is sufficient for thee."

That soul is now in the secret place of the Most High and sees in a new light the old truth: "Blessed is the man unto whom the Lord imputeth not iniquity!" (Psalm 32:2).

Verily, when the Lord does not impute unto him his iniquity, he has found refuge.

This old passage, too, takes on a new meaning: "Him that justifieth the ungodly" (Romans 4:5). Ungodly— that fits him. Never before has he seen it so clearly.

He experiences the greatest of all mysteries in Christianity, that of being *ungodly* and *just* at the same time.

Now promise after promise, the one more precious than the other, comes winging its way to his heart, like messengers from heaven. "There is therefore now no condemnation to them that are in Christ Jesus" (Romans 8:1).

Here we have the great mystery about the secret place of the Most High: *in Christ*.

As long as we are in Him, there is no condemnation to us. For as long as we are in Him, our iniquities are not imputed unto *us*. They have already once been imputed unto *Him*.

In Christ, his vicarious substitute, the sinner finds refuge and covert, from all sin and guilt, from all accusations and pangs of conscience.

Here these things cannot reach him.

No matter how he is accused and condemned by his own honest and sensitive heart, he turns to the blessed Savior and says, "I have nothing apart from Thee!"

And the Savior replies, "My grace is sufficient unto thee. I was made unto thee wisdom from God, and righteousness, and sanctification, and redemption."

The mystery of the Gospel begins to dawn upon his believing soul. He sees now that he is loved of God, not because of anything lovable in himself, but because God is love.

For no other reason.

Since God in love gave His Son as a ransom for sin, nothing can hinder God from receiving a sinner unto His loving heart, except this one thing, that he refuses to let Him do it.

As a little child really does nothing but let itself be loved, clothed, fed, washed, cared for, and caressed by its mother, so the sinner's unmerited and unfathomable privilege as a child of God is just this: To permit himself to be loved, cleansed, sanctified, fed, clothed, nurtured, and caressed by Almighty God.

And as the undeserved and untiring love of a mother is a helpless little child's refuge, shelter, and defense against all danger, both from within and without, so the unmerited love of God is the safe refuge which makes it possible for a frail and helpless child of God to move safely and unharmed among all the devils, all the wicked people, and all the temptations of the flesh in this world of sin and difficulty.

My refuge!

That is just the word. That is exactly what my rejoicing soul experiences. I can flee to God with everything. Therein lies our security.

A believing sinner has the privilege of fleeing to the Lord with everything, no matter what it may be.

It may be ever so small and insignificant, God will, nevertheless, intervene and help. No matter how great and difficult it may seem, God can bring it to pass for him.

If he gets into difficulty because of his old sinful habits—and that he does every day if he is a conscientious Christian—he no longer resorts to good resolves, which, of course, result in nothing but new disappointments and defeats. Nor does he permit himself to be driven into "despair and other sins," as Luther calls it.

Nay; he does as the young who creep under the wings of the mother-hen.

He flees to God, ashamed, humiliated, and undone. And he tells Him the whole truth: "Here I come again. I am in just as bad straits as I was last time. And this is happening so frequently that I am beginning to despair of myself utterly. I feel that it would be right of Thee to forsake me and never seek to help me any longer, I who am unfaithful toward Thee, undependable in spite of Thy loving care for me."

He experiences anew that the Lord is his refuge. "Can a woman forget her sucking child, that she should not have compassion on the son of her womb? Yea, these may forget, yet will not I forget thee. Behold, I have graven thee upon the palms of my hands." "Though your sins be as scarlet, they shall be as white as snow." "The blood of Jesus Christ, the Son of God, cleanseth from all sin."

Do not be afraid that God will grow weary of you

because you have gone down to defeat many times.
He who has begun the good work within you, will Himself perfect it unto the day of Jesus Christ. He is with
you, and suffers with you whenever you are defeated.
"He gives power to the faint; and to him that has no
might He increases strength."

Thus defeat becomes not only a *disappointment* but a
humiliation, which drives every honest believer the closer
to his Almighty Friend. And the more dependent he becomes upon his Savior, the more secure is his defense
against the overpowering temptations which assail him.

*

My refuge!

As we learn to know God, we flee to Him more and
more with our difficulties, temporal as well as spiritual.

There are times in our lives when our little life-boats
sail along quietly and smoothly. We encounter no difficulty with adverse winds and currents.

Our health is good. Our work prospers. Everything
goes along well in our homes; everything is peaceful and
congenial from day to day. Financially we get along well
also. Now and then we have a few difficulties, but on the
whole everything seems to work out wonderfully well.

In such times many Christians forget to go to the
secret place of the Most High.

Prosperous times make it easy to "believe" in God.
People think that God is good. Men give advice right
and left about believing in God.

Without a doubt, many a Christian has lost his spiritual
life in the sunny, but dry air of prosperity.

Only a few can weather prosperity and be none the
worse for it.

They are such as can do all things through Christ, who
strengtheneth them. Like Paul they have learned the
secret both to abound and to be in want (Philippians 4:

12-13). Their refuge is in the Lord in days of prosperity, as well as of adversity.

Nor do they fail to thank Him for it.

On the contrary, they give thanks to God for *all* things in the name of Jesus (Ephesians 5:20). And they are aware of their weaknesses even when they are prosperous.

Therefore, too, they flee to God even in prosperity.

Thus they overcome the world, even its prosperity.

*

There are other times in our lives when adverse winds and storms let loose their fury against our little skiff. All our plans are crossed; all our hopes are dashed to pieces.

Illness, sorrow, and the vacant chair find their way into our homes. Impaired health makes work a burden and leaves us in straightened financial circumstances.

One difficulty follows hard upon the other. There is scarcely time to catch one's breath between the breakers.

Then it is well to know the way to the secret place of the Most High. Blessed is he who has learned to flee to God, to seek refuge under His wings, and to find a haven from storm and tempest.

Two and a half thousand years ago they sang:

"God is our refuge and strength, a very present help in trouble" (Psalm 46:1).

Yea, verily, in times of *trouble* our refuge in the Lord has always been a very present help. When the soul which is sick and weary unto death creeps under the wings of the loving Savior and speaks out its woe, or sinks down in nameless anguish without uttering a word, then it experiences what Jesus promised His friends: "My peace I give unto you. Not as the world giveth, give I unto you" (John 14:27).

Not as the world giveth!

The peace which the world gives endures only as long as prosperity lasts; it fades away at the mere thought of future adversity.

Jesus, on the other hand, possessed a peace which could not be shaken by adversity, suffering, or death.

And it is *His* peace that Jesus promises to give us.

The peace which abides in the darkest night of adversity, which is so unexplainably strong that believing souls no longer even ask God to remove their affliction.

This peace involves a struggle, it is true.

We all shrink from suffering, sorrow, and affliction, and are inclined to pray God continually to remove our difficulties from us. But when we in our helplessness finally rest our hearts, weary, rebellious, and averse to suffering as they may be, upon the Savior's breast, then the great miracle takes place: He gives us *His* peace.

The peace which is not disturbed by adversity and which rejoices to make the words of Jesus its own: "The cup which the Father hath given me, shall I not drink it?" (John 18:11).

Not until then does one experience fully what it means to sit in the shadow of the Most High. Not until then does one experience the truth of the words of the ancient psalmist: "In the day of trouble he will keep me secretly in his pavilion: In the covert of his tabernacle will he hide me; he will lift me up upon a rock" (Psalm 27:5).

Verily, upon a rock!

We have at last found solid ground upon which to place our feet.

Our peace and our joy are no longer dependent upon the many outward things. We find rest in God, and leave it to the pierced hands of the Savior whether we are to be prosperous or not.

Upon a rock!

Here we are afforded a new and remarkable *outlook*.

We see our own lives and the world in general in a different light.

Our past life especially stands out in remarkably clear relief. Things which we before had not thought about a great deal, or things which we had thought about a great deal but never understood, we now see in the clear super-light of eternity.

And they become sacred and dear to us.

As for our own lives, which appear to others like chaotic conglomerations of conflicting misfortunes and failures, and which we ourselves a short time ago looked upon in the same light, there too we now see the unseen hand which is guiding all things. We feel His warm hand-clasp and can sing quietly and confidently:

"Sometimes 'mid scenes of deepest gloom,
Sometimes where Eden's bowers bloom.
By waters still, o'er troubled sea,—
Still 'tis His hand that leadeth me!

"He leadeth me, He leadeth me,
By His own hand He leadeth me:
His faithful follower I would be,
For by His hand He leadeth me."

*

Of course, it does happen that suffering, sorrowing, and oppressed souls now and then become weary to death of the billows of adversity which beat upon them, one after the other.

Their aching souls cry out, *"Why all this sorrow and suffering and tribulation?"*

The answer is, "To *teach* us to flee to God."

To do so is an art.

And every art must be practised if proficiency in it is to be acquired. To flee to God is without question the highest art in life. And it is by no means easy to learn.

But God helps us by sending us suffering and tribulation.

Tribulation makes us weary of the ways of the world and thereby enables us the more easily to choose the way of life.

Most of us do not learn to know what the world is really like until it turns its wrong side toward us and we cut ourselves upon its sharply protruding edges.

Not until then do we learn to desist from proud words and haughty bearing. Not until we have been plucked to the skin of all our feathers do we seek refuge in our helplessness in the secret place of the Most High.

What we then experience often becomes determining for the rest of our lives. The reality, the depth, and the riches of grace which we then experience give us a personal acquaintanceship with our Lord which come to mean something to us also when our troubles are over.

We have learned the art, the secret, of taking refuge under His wings. We have begun to see that this is the simple solution of *all* of life's problems.

When I have taken a difficulty into the secret place of the Most High, I have really already overcome it, even though there are things about it which I as yet do not understand.

We begin to see that *this* is the victory which overcomes the world.

The spiritual atmosphere of the world is so frigid that it cools every regenerate heart unless that heart has learned to take refuge incessantly in the secret place of the Most High, there to be warmed by the heart of Jesus, even as the young of the mother-hen creep under her wings and are warmed.

In this sinful world, where everything is permeated by sin, it is wholly impossible to live a life in God unless we unceasingly seek refuge under His wings.

He who learns to take refuge in this secret place thereby also enters quietly and naturally into the right attitude, becomes properly orientated, toward all of life's relationships.

To *experience God* day by day is all that is necessary in order to be clear as to what to do and thus be right in all of life's relationships.

Experience God, I say; not only think about God, long for God, or talk about God.

My dear reader! If your Christianity consists essentially of thinking, longing, or talking, then seek refuge with all of this in the secret place of the Most High. Lay it all before Him, ask Him once again to forgive you for being unfaithful, for the sake of the shed blood of Jesus Christ, and to take you to His heart.

> "I take, O cross, thy shadow
> For my abiding place;
> I ask no other sunshine than
> The sunshine of His face;
> Content to let the world go by,
> To know no gain or loss,
> My sinful self my only shame,
> My glory all the cross."

*

"He that dwelleth in the secret place of the Most High . . . will say of Jehovah, He is my refuge."

He will *say* it.

The psalmist reminds us here that it is normal to say this of Jehovah, or *to* Jehovah, as it is also translated. We should take particular notice of this. For it seems to me that most of us say very little about *this* to the Lord.

We pray, yea, verily, we pray often. And we pray for many good things, both for ourselves and for others, which is all well and good.

But our conversation with the Lord should also include this of which the psalmist here speaks. We should say unto the Lord, "Thou art my refuge and my fortress."

Of course, we may say it in our own way and in our own words, if that comes more natural.

But we should *say* it.

In other words, this should be included in the things about which we speak to the Lord when we are alone with Him, either when we are in our secret chamber, or during the course of the day while we are working or resting.

In other words, it is *important* that we say it.

It is of importance to God. It is His *desire* that we should say to Him, Thou art my refuge, my fortress. It is His desire that we should tell Him what He is to us. It is His desire that we should thank and praise Him.

We so easily overlook and forget this aspect of God.

We think of God as being so great and exalted that He has no heart, no feelings, and that it means nothing to Him whether we thank Him or not.

But in this we are thoroughly mistaken. God's is the warmest heart in the great All. And no one has a finer or more tender emotional life than He.

No one is made happy more easily than God.

This, too, Jesus has shown us.

Behold His joy at the one leper who had been cleansed and who returned and gave thanks for his healing. Read once more the brief account in Luke 17:11-19, and you will see how happy the Samaritan made Jesus merely by turning back, falling upon his face, and giving thanks.

Why did this make Jesus rejoice so exceedingly?

The answer to this I find most readily in verse eighteen: "Were there none found that returned to give glory to God, save this stranger?"

To Jesus, to give thanks means to give *glory to God*. To God be the glory! It means something to God when we return and give thanks. And therefore it means something to God when we who are in the secret place of the Most High say unto Him, Thou art my refuge, my fortress!

In the next place, it means something *to us*.

Our prayers contain as a rule too much *begging*.

Not that we pray too much and that God becomes weary of us. Nay, Jesus has by a number of parables sought to impress upon us that we should pray with boldness (Luke 11:5-8; 18:1-8).

Where we err is in thanking Him too little.

Our prayers become so full of begging that we have no place for thanksgiving and praise. There is too little desire in our hearts to thank God and sing His praises.

This not only grieves God; it also imperils our prayer life, in fact our whole Christian life.

Nothing gives us more courage and confidence when we pray than to see the answers to prayer that we have already received, and to thank God for them. We not only gain courage, but also a new desire to pray for more.

And, most important of all, we grow in that childlike *faith* which is the condition of answered prayer.

"He that dwelleth in the secret place of the Most High . . . will say of Jehovah, He is my refuge."

This is more than thanksgiving. This is praise. For we praise Him when we give expression to what He is and does.

And we need to learn how to praise God; the people of our day have almost forgotten that.

*

Most people flee, not *to* God but *from* God.

Strange as it seems, men fear no one as much as God. That is also why most people in this world keep away from God entirely, and from everything associated with the Divine.

If we should tell these people that they take the attitude they do because they are *afraid,* they would undoubtedly protest strongly. Instead of admitting that this was the case they would advance a long list of other reasons for staying away from Christ.

However, when these same people become awakened spiritually and begin to search their hearts, we notice that they soon realize and quickly acknowledge that their innermost reason for staying away from God was fear.

It is perhaps not always so much fear of punishment as it is fear lest religion should mar or perhaps even completely destroy their happiness in life.

That is why they postpone becoming religious, usually until they become sick or aged—when they have no more happiness in life to look forward to anyway.

Others again are apparently not so afraid of God as that

They are religious. They seek God, go to church, and have devotions at home, at least now and then.

But that many of them, too, are really afraid of God becomes very apparent every time that they happen to hear a Biblical and authoritative message about conversion and the new birth. Immediately they set about to defend themselves against such thoughts with all the intensity of the urge of self-preservation. They have an instinctive fear that such thoughts are dangerous.

Is not everything perfectly right and proper between them and God? Have they not, practically speaking, made an agreement with Him with which both He and they are satisfied? In other words, they are using their religiosity as a means of keeping away from God.

How afraid they are of God becomes quickly apparent when they are told that they must be converted. Immediately God becomes to them the greatest of all dangers. For to be told that they must be converted constitutes an attack upon that thing in their lives with which they least of all desire to part, and which they thought they had saved for themselves by their religiosity, namely, the privilege of living a *self-directed* life. To sacrifice a little religiosity to God, that they can do; but when He demands that they be converted and surrender their self-directed lives to Him, then they begin to look upon Him immediately as their most dangerous enemy.

That is why religious people of this type oppose and condemn positive and evangelical preaching of conversion and the new birth, why they, in spite of their religiosity and churchliness, simply stay away even from their own church if they must listen to preaching of this kind when they come.

Such is the heart of man.

Almost two thousand years ago the Scriptures described it as follows: "The mind of the flesh is enmity against God" (Romans 8:7). But men will not believe this. And for that reason they think of the most unheard of excuses when trying to explain why they do not surrender their lives to God.

Everybody else is to blame but themselves.

Should I by these words be reaching some one who has hidden away from God, and by the means I have described sought to shield himself from His insistent and persistent call, to such a one I would bring a greeting from the Word of God.

It is the authoritative message which the ancient prophet once brought from God to His rebellious people:

"It is thy destruction, O Israel, that thou art against me, against thy help" (Hosea 13:9).

If you would sit down and quietly reflect a little, you would see how this word of prophecy would throw light upon your life.

It is perhaps not difficult for you to point to a series

of misfortunes which have befallen you and made your life dark and dreary, misfortunes for some of which you yourself were to blame as well as misfortunes for which you yourself think you were not to blame. Some of them have already receded into the distant past and no longer oppress you as they did before. Others are like open wounds that will not heal.

Listen, my friend, to what the Lord thinks about your life and your misfortunes.

He sees them all—more clearly than you do. But to Him they can all be summed up in this one great misfortune: "Thou art against me, against thy help."

And within your own bosom there is a still, small voice which says:

"That is true. The tragedy of my life is that I have always been against God."

This still, small voice has not always been permitted to speak. As a rule you would not listen to it. You knew very well what to do in order to silence it. And you made use of those means.

But occasionally you did not succeed. You still heard the still, small voice within. And serious moments they were. For it was God Himself who spoke to you through that voice. What He said was spoken seriously and with authority, but withal in tones of wondrous love. Something soft and tender entered into your heart, bringing into your life many fine longings and high hopes. And many good resolves. You were *almost a Christian.*

But nothing more came of it.

Your fervent emotions and longings soon subsided. You became more afraid of God than ever, and fled farther and farther away from Him.

You *had* to do that. For "he that is not with me is against me," says Jesus.

Since then you have continued to flee away from Him. But from the great misfortune of your life you could not flee. And your continued flight only continues to add to your unhappiness.

My dear friend, flee *to* God, and do it now.

Tell Him about the great tragedy of your life. Seek refuge with all your sins and all your rebelliousness *under His wings*.

There you will find what you need: rest for your weary soul.

> Other refuge have I none;
>   Hangs my helpless soul on **Thee**;
> Leave, ah, leave me not alone,
>   Still support and comfort me
> All my trust on Thee is stayed;
>   All my help from Thee I bring;
> Cover my defenseless head
>   With the shadow of Thy wing.

In the Day of Trouble

*"In the covert of his tabernacle will he hide me;
he will lift me up upon a rock."*
—Psalm 27:5.

IT is not easy to live in this world of ours. It is full
of people who, according to the Scriptures and our
own experience, are wicked. These wicked people
cannot, of course, avoid being wicked toward one
another. As a result the world is full of suffering, inflicted
by one person upon another. Married folk upon each
other. Brothers and sisters upon one another. Friend
upon friend. Neighbor upon neighbor. Acquaintance
upon acquaintance. Stranger upon stranger.

Can we then expect to get through this world without
experiencing evil at the hands of some one? No, that is
quite impossible, unthinkable.

If we would reconcile ourselves to this fact, it would
undoubtedly be easier for us to endure misunderstanding,
to bear with patience the envy, the cutting words, the
affronts, the slander, the opposition, and the persecution
of men.

Not even among devout Christians can we avoid trouble
of this kind. Some evil attaches to every believer on
earth.

And at some unguarded point or other in his life this
evil will crop out, also in his associations with others.

Believers, too, can be exceedingly mean to each other,
both in thought, word, and deed. Moreover, nothing

hurts us as much as when Christian people are unkind toward us.

When they misunderstand and misinterpret what we do, when they slander or cast aspersions upon our person, deep wounds are inflicted upon our souls. This soon gives rise to sore and bitter thoughts.

There are perhaps few things that are so hard, so difficult, for us to learn as to endure to be misunderstood and opposed by Christian men and women.

When David had sinned against the Lord by numbering the people and was to be punished for doing so, God permitted him to choose whether he wanted to flee three months before his foes while they pursued him or that there should be a three days' pestilence in his land.

To which the old, experienced king replied, "I am in a great strait: let us fall now into the hand of Jehovah; for his mercies are great; and let me not fall into the hand of man" (2 Samuel 24:13-14).

Our lot is not always an easy one when we fall into the hand of man. But at some time or other in life this usually happens.

Never are we more helpless than then.

Sorrow and adversity and tribulation can be hard enough to bear. But as long as men understand us and sympathize with us we feel that we have remarkable strength to bear it all.

But when men neither sympathize with us nor understand us, then we experience a choky feeling, as when we cannot get air.

Job's worst experience, too, was when his friends treated him the way they did. That was when his cup of woe ran over, and he murmured against both God and men.

At such a time we turn away from men and to the living God.

We begin to realize what it means when men "make flesh their arm." When tempests of this kind break loose, it is unspeakably blessed to take quiet refuge in the secret place of the Most High. And feel that He understands us even though everybody else misunderstands.

Then it is blessed to lay before the Lord the deepest and innermost motives of our hearts, and to let Him examine them one by one. And to accept His disapproval of everything we did which was unclean and selfish, but also to experience His approval of everything that we did in love toward Him and in the service of our fellow men.

Then our position becomes so strong and so secure that we can bear the misunderstanding and opposition of our fellow beings.

O how blessed it is that the Lord has a tabernacle in which to hide us in the day of trouble!

"He will lift me up upon a rock."

From this rock there is a glorious view. Among other things a benign light falls upon the people round about us. We begin to look upon them in the light of God's love.

Which enables us to *understand* them.

Furthermore, we see ourselves in them. We recall that that is how we, too, have frequently treated our fellow men. We did not realize until afterwards that we had wronged them.

Upon this rock, too, we experience an exalted joy. For once we are really *better* than people think we are.

Before, the opposite was usually the case. Men thought highly of us. But we who knew our own innermost selves knew that they attributed to us nobler motives than we really possessed.

How emancipating it is to know that I really possess something more and better than people think I do.

That is what we experience when the Lord hides us in the covert of His tabernacle in the day of trouble.

"He will lift me up upon a rock!"

Up there we have a wide view. I have already mentioned some of the things we see from this vantage point. May I mention a few more?

We see what David saw in the day of his deepest humiliation, when he said that God had commanded Shimei to curse him. (2 Samuel 16:10.)

We see the invisible hand of God back of the harsh judgments of inconsiderate men.

And we experience some of that unexplainable security which the secret place of the Most High affords to trembling souls.

Our Earthly Calling

"Even so let your light shine before men; that they may see your good works, and glorify your Father who is in heaven."

—MATTHEW 5:16.

THIS is a very difficult chapter. Not to write, but to practice in life. In all religions it has been most difficult to assign the earthly calling its proper place. As a rule life has been divided into two parts, the religious and the secular.

The *religious* part has been made to include everything that pertained to the divine, namely, worship in all its various forms, sacrifices, ablutions, fastings, prayers, and so forth.

The rest of life has constituted the *secular* part.

About it the gods were not really concerned. When they were punctiliously accorded the sacrifices and the worship due to them, they were satisfied, and did not concern themselves about men's daily lives.

That was a matter which concerned the family and the state.

It was not only the *heathen* religions which had a tendency to assign the daily life and the earthly calling to a place *outside* of religion.

In ancient *Israel* we find something similar.

There was nothing that the prophets reproved more sharply than that men were punctilious in the matter of divine worship, but lived in open immorality. "I cannot away with iniquity and the solemn meeting" (Isaiah 1:13). See also Amos 4:1, 4, 5.

Jesus rebuked the *Pharisees* for the same thing.

They were zealous and scrupulous in things *religious*. They gave a tithe even of such inconsequential things as mint, anise, and cummin, which they raised in their little garden plots. They prayed long prayers. They compassed land and sea to make one proselyte. They cleansed the outside of the cup and of the platter.

But they left *morals* as they were.

They devoured widows' houses and left undone the weightier matters of the law, justice, and mercy. Within they were full from extortion and excess. (Matthew 23:14, 23, 25.)

We find the same faulty relation between morality and religion among the Jews to this very day.

I remember the first time a Jew visited our home. He was a transient peddler.

My mother was a great friend of the Jews, and was very happy to have one in her home. And because she earnestly desired to make a festive occasion out of the visit of this member of God's own chosen people at her home, she had, among other things, prepared some really good waffles for him.

But when he was seated at the table, she could not get him to even taste them. He could not speak a great deal of Norwegian, but in his broken language he could say, "Schweinefett, Schweinefett."

"No," said mother, "there is no fat of pork in these waffles at all; they are made of butter."

But it did not help. He would not taste them. With a skeptical smile he kept on repeating his: "Schweinefett."

So punctilious could he be when it came to observing the Mosaic law against eating pork.

But to cheat people with his miserable wares and his exorbitant prices, that he could do at every farm home, without the least compunction!

This faulty relationship between morality and religion we find also within the *Christian Church*.

In all denominations, too.

Men observe worship, the sacraments, the holy days, and all the other religious customs and ceremonies. But morality, everyday living, lags far behind.

The worst of all is that men really think that it is possible to serve God in this way.

This erroneous relationship between morality and religion we find even among *believing Christians*. The heathen raises his head among them, too, and divides life into two parts: one religious, the other secular.

The work which we do specifically *for God* becomes a thing by itself; our daily life, our earthly calling, another.

Men do not see that our daily life, our daily work, is the most important part of the work we do for God.

Then, too, we have the incongruity between *Sunday* and *everyday,* between life as it is lived in the *home* and life as it is lived in religious *meetings*.

We find husbands and wives who at home flare up in anger, have violent tempers, or are gloomy and grouchy; but outside of the home are godly and zealous and willing to make sacrifices for Christ.

Then, too, we find children who at home are contrary, difficult to manage, and contentious and irritable in their relations with their brothers and sisters; but who are zealous workers in religious societies, meetings, and prayer services. Perhaps they even sing, testify, and preach.

We find men in responsible positions who in their daily lives are peevish and imperious and in whom their subordinates observe very little conscientiousness, not to speak of Christianity. Even less do they see of any zeal for the salvation of the immortal souls in their employ.

But outside, in Christian organizations of various kinds, these men are zealous for the salvation of souls, evangelism, and many other such things.

Then again we find employees who studiously avoid doing more work than they are strictly compelled to do. Clock-watchers and time-stealers. Difficult to get along with. They will not stand corrected, and become pouty and peevish upon the least provocation. Their superiors see little conscientiousness on their part again, and even less zeal for the immortal souls with whom they are associated from day to day. Nothing in their daily lives gives evidence of a desire to *win* their superiors for Christ.

But they, too, are often zealous in such special Christian enterprises as the Sunday school, the ladies' aid societies, choirs and other musical organizations, evangelistic meetings, prayer meetings, and after-meetings.

They live their lives on two planes, a religious and a secular.

I am reminded of a little incident from my childhood.

We were hauling sand. And even though I was not a very big lad, I was along—was even driving a horse all by myself.

We had just come to the sand-pit early one cold winter morning. Many others were hauling at the same time. But we were the first ones at the pit on this particular morning and were therefore entitled to load up where it was easiest to get the sand.

But right behind us came another man. He sized up the situation at once, came over to where I was, and said in a friendly way, "You are such a little fellow, I'll help you turn your horse around."

Whereupon he deliberately drove my vehicle into another intake, and took for himself the best place, to which I was entitled.

I was, of course, only a little fellow, and did not dare to say anything about what a grown-up man did.

But how surprised and indignant I was!

That man stood up and testified at meetings on Sunday. And on Monday morning he could do a thing like that!

He continued to preach. But every time I heard him, he accomplished little more, as far as I was concerned, than to bring to my mind the recollection of that Monday morning in the sand-pit.

Permit me to mention another incident. It, too, happens to be about hauling sand.

A relative of mine came driving along the road one day and met one of his neighbors. "But Peter, my friend," he said to his neighbor, "are you working your piece of road now? Have you not heard that they are re-allocating the road work, and that there is very little likelihood that you will get exactly the same piece that you now have?"

In reply Peter straightened up his back, which was bent with labor, wiped the perspiration from his brow, and replied: "Yes, I heard the other day that they were planning to re-allocate the road work; and that is just why I want to get my old piece in good shape. I want the man who gets this piece after I have had it to get a piece that is in good condition."

To which my relative commented as follows: "I had for a long time been in doubt about Christianity and the Christians, but that day I became convinced that there was at least one Christian in the world."

He had met a man who served *God* in the midst of his daily work. To him this was a stronger testimony than could ever be given in words or in meetings.

Our great temptation—and it is common to us all—is to neglect *everyday Christianity*. It is far easier for us to lay the emphasis upon Sunday Christianity.

All of us labor under this temptation.

And, as far as I am able to understand, our age labors under it more than previous ages. I think that this is due to organization.

The organized Christian work of our day is so many-sided and requires so much time and effort that we inadvertently give it first place in our consciousness.

It *need* not be so. I do not make mention of this for the purpose of chiming in with that chorus of criticism which is being directed against organization and organizations at the present time. All I say is that it can very easily develop that way.

It is important, therefore, for us Christians in these days to see what the *Bible* says about our earthly calling.

Permit me to mention three passages which are especially clear:

"Whether therefore ye eat, or drink, or whatsoever ye do, do all to the glory of God" (1 Corinthians 10:31).

"And whatsoever ye do, in word or in deed, do all in the name of the Lord Jesus, giving thanks to God the Father through him" (Colossians 3:17).

"Even so let your light shine before men; that they may see your good works, and glorify your Father who is in heaven" (Matthew 5:16).

These three passages tell us, in the first place, that everything we do should be done in Jesus' name and to the glory of God.

In the next place, the Lord promises us in these passages that if our daily lives are a spiritual service of good works, we will thereby become instruments unto the salvation of our fellow men.

That is what He means when He says that they shall praise God when they see our good works.

We find this thought expressed still more clearly in one of Peter's epistles:

"In like manner, ye wives, be in subjection to your own husbands; that, even if any obey not the word, they may without the word be gained by the behavior of their wives; beholding your chaste behavior coupled with fear" (1 Peter 3:1-2).

Here believing wives are promised that their unbelieving husbands shall be won for God *without words* by the daily lives of the wives, the husbands beholding their chaste behavior coupled with fear and their meek and quiet spirit, which is in the sight of God of great price.

The apostle uses a word in this connection which I think we should especially note, namely, the word *beholding*. He wants to tell us, no doubt, that nothing in our Christian life is stronger or more effective than that part of it which others can behold with their eyes.

We, on the other hand, seem to have an unshakable faith in words.

But the apostle says here that the unbelievers who cannot be won by words, whether they be Sunday words or everyday words, can be won by everyday Christianity, Christianity which they can behold before their very eyes every day of their lives.

*

These Scripture passages afford us an insight into what the Bible teaches regarding a Christian's daily life and earthly calling.

They should be a divine service, a service for God.

This is of great price in the sight of God.

And it is a means of bringing salvation to those of our fellow men who are the very hardest to win.

This exalted view of our earthly calling did not, however, maintain itself very long after the apostolic age.

In the Roman Catholic Church this Biblical view has been completely suppressed. Ordinary, secular work is to Roman Catholics not holy but unholy.

If a Roman Catholic desires to do something *for God*, something with which God will be well pleased, then he must do something *extra*, something outside of his regular earthly calling.

To marry and establish a Christian home is not holy and well-pleasing to God; to enter a monastery and live a celibate life is.

To be a *mother* is not holy; to be a *nun* is.

To do one's daily work is not holy; but to make pilgrimages, to fast, recite prayers, and make donations to churches and convents, and so forth, is.

Here, too, *Luther* brought out the Biblical view again, namely, that it is the heart to which God looks. Therefore we cannot say that certain acts are holy in themselves while others *per se* are not holy.

Everything we do is well-pleasing to God when we do it in the right spirit, that is, in Jesus' name and to the glory of God, in grateful love toward God and in sacrificial zeal for the salvation of our fellow men.

God does not, therefore, judge our work according to its outward prestige and glory. Nor according to its dimensions or outward success, its results. He does not look to see if we have been successful or not, if we have succeeded in accomplishing much or little. He looks to the spirit in which we do our work.

Which means that He looks to our *faithfulness*.

Therefore, as Luther says, it is just as well pleasing to God to sweep the floor as it is to preach the Gospel, provided we do both in the right spirit.

And he says further that whether we are to preach or

to sweep is simply a question of *gifts of grace*. And these the Spirit divides unto each one severally as He wills. (1 Corinthians 12:11).

Here man's earthly calling is brought back to its Biblical place as the most important part of the believer's service unto God.

However, the Roman Catholic view quickly re-asserted itself. If anything was to be done *for God,* it had to be something extra, something *outside* of one's daily occupation.

I remember a young servant girl whom I met a number of years ago. She had been converted at one of my meetings. And what a miserable conversion it was! I knew the family for whom she worked. They were Christian people, and were kind to the girl. Of course, they were happy at the thought that she had been converted.

But to their great regret they found that her conversion had produced no change in her daily life. She was the same slouch in her work that she had always been, as frivolous of speech as ever, and as vain in her manner of dress as before. Besides, she was just as peevish and just as much of a pouter as she had always been.

I spoke to her very seriously about this a couple of times. Apparently she took it very nicely. But there was no change for the better.

After some time I met her again.

With beaming face she came up to me and said, "Now I have really given myself up to God."

"O, have you," I replied. "Have you finally become truly *converted* and given God His way in your daily life and taken up the struggle against the sins which you hitherto have refused to do battle against?"

The joyful expression on her face vanished, and in a tone of somewhat diminished ardor she answered, "I have given myself to the Salvation Army."

To give herself to God, also to her, meant to do something *extra*. But the sacrifice which God expected of her and about which He had spoken to her every day since the time of her spiritual awakening, the sacrifice of her old sinful habits—about that she would hear nothing.

I mention this because it illustrates typically how we Protestants also, in spite of Luther, have introduced into our thinking the Roman Catholic separation between religion and morality, between work for God and our earthly calling.

*

It was remarkable that Hans Nielsen Hauge also found the way back to Luther on this point.

Hauge and his friends laid the chief emphasis upon every-day Christianity.

Least of all were they Sunday Christians.

Festive gatherings, functions of various kinds, and organization were, on the whole, not in their line.

But they were, in lieu of this, the better versed along certain other lines.

In the first place, they lived Christ in their daily lives. This was to them the way in which the genuineness of conversion was to be demonstrated. That is why they were so conscientious and strict with themselves.

In the second place, they were cognizant of the fact that their daily lives and their daily work were their real spiritual service, that is, their work *for God*.

This was their first and foremost way of bringing their fellow men under the influence of the Word, and thus winning them for the Lord.

It was this, too, that made their lives a divine benediction and filled them with deep earnestness. They felt that if they were to win for God the people with whom they associated day by day, and not repel them, they must be very conscientious with respect to the way they lived their daily lives.

Their "chaste behaviour coupled with fear" gained the day for them. Not words. The old Haugeans were not men of many words. They even prayed in one of their hymns that they might be "richer in deed than word."

In the third place, they knew how to make their earthly calling promote the cause of brotherly love.

Hauge himself took the lead in this respect by starting enterprises of various kinds in different parts of the country and thus helping the needy brethren to provide for themselves.

If any of the believing brethren ever became destitute, their Haugean friends would help them get work of one kind or another and thus prevent them from being compelled to accept charity at the hands of others.

This *social* aspect of Haugeanism, this practical and wise form of helpfulness, aroused great interest and won the respect of even the most bitter enemies of the movement.

*

It is a well known fact that the Haugeans were diligent in their earthly calling.

They were capable farmers, craftsmen, business men, factory owners, and men of affairs. They were pioneers in many fields, and took a prominent part in the rehabilitation of their country after the years of distress which preceded and followed the year 1814.

But not only that.

The greatest thing of all was that they succeeded in accomplishing this without injuring or weakening their inner life with God. Theirs was an unspotted shield. They had not paid for their material success with evil consciences, with means which could not abide the light.

This was the *great strength* of the Haugeans.

The secret of it was no doubt the fact that from the very beginning they took the right attitude toward their earthly calling. They looked upon their daily tasks as the most important part of their work for the Lord.

As the strength of Haugeanism declined, the life of its adherents also sank to a lower level in this respect. From then on we begin to see these able men become an easy prey of their temporal affairs. An atmosphere of the worldly and of the earth-bound enveloped them. Many of them, too, became exceedingly niggardly and miserly.

*

There are two dangers, two difficulties in particular, connected with our earthly calling.

One is to be shiftless and slovenly when working for others.

The extent to which this acts as a hindrance to the salvation of the unconverted is so great, as I see it, that it is difficult to exaggerate it.

There is a large and steadily increasing number of people who, practically speaking, never hear the Word of God, and who, therefore, never come in contact with Christianity, except through the Christian men and women whom they employ in their homes, their factories, their stores, or their offices.

And you can be sure these people use their eyes.

As they have a right to do.

For Christ says that men shall see our good works.

Young Christian friends!

You who in one way or another are employed by unconverted people, God give you eyes to see the work which you have to do for Him each day. It is your daily life which can, and which should, win back to God these people who are so far away from Him.

It is well that we have pastors. But when the pastors cannot get these people to sit beneath their pulpits?

It is well that we have evangelists. But when people never set foot in a place where an evangelist is speaking?

Young friends! Here you have a work to do which no pastor or evangelist can do.

You can most certainly not do it by *words*. You will soon learn that. And then it is good to have the divine promise about winning them without the word by your chaste behavior coupled with fear, by a meek and quiet spirit, which is of great price in the sight of both God and man.

It will not be an easy task. On the contrary, it will tax your patience exceedingly.

Nevertheless, do your daily work without dissimulation and slovenliness; do it diligently and in love, because the Lord expects it of you. He needs you in the work of His kingdom, needs you as present and positive proof of the fact that Christianity *transforms* people, not on Sundays only but in their daily lives, in their daily work.

The second danger in connection with our daily work is that of being consumed by one's earthly tasks, especially when one is in business for himself.

The desire for gain and profit often takes the upper hand completely. One ceases to work *for the Lord* and looks upon the whole thing as his own, even though one is generous at times and gives to the Lord a little of that which one otherwise regards as one's personal possessions.

Just as soon as our daily work ceases to be a service for God, we no longer see the immortal souls with which we are associated from day to day. We no longer treat them as souls which we ought to try to win for the Lord.

Least of all do we see that these are the very ones

whom God would first and foremost have us win for Him.

*

My impression is that a new Christian type is being developed in our day.

As I see it, it is being developed in connection with our various Christian organizations.

It is without doubt a characteristic phenomenon of our age and is found not only in Norway, but in Sweden, Denmark, and America as well, as far as my experience goes.

This type comprises Christian men who are capable and efficient in their earthly calling, oftentimes exceedingly capable. They are interested in God's cause, too; in fact, they often show much willingness to sacrifice and great zeal for the salvation of others. Some of them are intent upon having evangelistic meetings continually.

But, strange enough, they do not manifest the same zeal and interest in their daily work. All their Christian work and all their Christian interest is centered in their organization, in which they are exceedingly active.

Their attitude reminds one of a well known practice in connection with the border patrol.

As soon as one who has reached the age of military service has served once on the border patrol, he can furnish a "substitute." That is, a man can hire some one to take his place, so that he himself will not be called upon to serve any longer.

The Christian people to whom I am referring are so busy with their profitable earthly tasks that they have not time to serve the Lord in their daily lives.

So they hire substitutes.

They help to pay evangelists and traveling secretaries to do the work of the Lord throughout the cities and villages of the land. Not that they themselves are inactive.

On the contrary, they love to attend evangelistic meetings, especially the after-meetings. *There* they are zealous for the salvation of souls, in fact, often so zealous that they are almost dangerous to have around.

But in their daily lives they show no such zeal whatsoever for those in their employ, or for those with whom they otherwise come in contact in their daily work. On the contrary, they are often a hindrance to the salvation of such because of their harshness, selfishness, and their clever way of being unreliable in business dealings.

We must pray God to deliver us from this.

For this would mean the death of Christianity if it were allowed to spread.

Let us try to find our way back to the old paths, to the every-day Christianity of the old Haugeans, with their circumspect and dependable daily lives.

That is what the world is sighing for today.

It has had enough of words.

*

We are all no doubt aware of the difficulties in this connection.

When we see how almost everything that is called Christianity instinctively tends to become associated with the extra work of the church or some subsidiary Christian organization, and how hard it is for people to look upon their daily lives and earthly callings as a service *for God,* we are easily tempted to become discouraged.

But that must not be.

Let us instead go to God and *pray* for ourselves and for one another. And then let us *speak* to one another about this matter, privately and in public meetings. Let us also encourage and admonish one another along these lines.

When once we begin to turn our eyes in this direction, when once we set this as the goal of our Christian life, we will find that we will succeed. Even though it will take time.

Of course, it will mean a *struggle!*

For there is nothing that Old Adam is so afraid of as every-day Christianity.

Neither is there anything that Satan fears so much.

I do not think that he has anything against meetings, whether we have many meetings or big meetings or "good" meetings, as long as he sees that meetings consume most of our interest and effort; that Christianity no longer permeates our daily, workaday lives, does not become our first, our primary, our essential service for God.

There was a funeral in town.

A Christian man was dead. He was known far and wide, and a large number of his many and faithful friends were assembled for the rites. At his bier many expressed their gratitude to God for what this servant of the Lord had been and had accomplished.

Finally the oldest son stepped forward to the edge of the grave and thanked everybody for the love they had shown his father while he lived and for the honors they had paid him at the funeral.

After which he added:

"I, too, desire to say a few words about father today. Father was a Christian at *home.* That is to me greater than all the good things that have been said here today about father's life and work."

In other words, the departed one was one who knew that Christianity should first and last be *every-day Christianity.*

The Fear of God

"Work out your own salvation with fear and trembling; for it is God who worketh in you both to will and to work, for his good pleasure."
—Philippians 2:12-13.

THIS is a profound, a deep saying. And far be it from me to think that I am capable of sounding its depths or expounding its riches. But that part of this passage which I *am* able to grasp makes it exceedingly precious to me.

The clearest part of this profound saying is the conclusion: "It is God who worketh in you both to will and to work."

Listen to this, in particular you who have begun to convert yourselves, but have not succeeded. You have learned that conversion is a change of heart, which is just what you have not been able to accomplish.

Your heart is as full of selfish, vain, begrudging, bitter, and unclean thoughts as ever. Your *desire* is toward sin, even though you struggle against it. Your desire is *not* toward God. You must compel yourself to pray and read the Bible. And when you occasionally do what you think is the will of God, you do so very unwillingly.

Listen to the secret which the apostle has to confide to you: "It is God who worketh in you both to will and to work, for his good pleasure."

This is a great secret and of decisive importance in connection with the salvation and the peace of your soul.

God does *not* expect you to have the power to change your heart by the power of your own will, and thus enable you to hate sin and love God.

He does *not* expect you to be able to press out of your own heart a desire to pray or read the Word of God, nor does He expect you to be able with a willing mind to serve Him and sacrifice and suffer for Him.

Of you He expects only this one thing, that you tell Him the truth, tell Him the situation as it is with reference to the attitude of your heart and the life you are living.

Moreover, you cannot even do *this* of yourself.

It is God who must work also this. He it is who must tell you this truth. Of yourself you cannot even see the truth about yourself. It is He who by His Spirit must convince you in such a way that you not only *know* the truth, but also are inwardly, personally convinced that you are as sinful as the Spirit of God says you are.

That you desire to be converted—that, too, God has worked within you.

The Scriptures say that God *gives* repentance and remission of sins (Acts 5:31). He gives repentance by working in your will until you freely and without compulsion desire to become penitent.

That God succeeded in making you penitent was no easy task either, as far as that is concerned.

When He first began to work in your will, you would not yield. You resisted Him—perhaps for a long time. You tried in many ways to rid yourself of the influence which the will of God had begun to exert upon you.

But God did not give up. He continued to work in your will until its opposition ceased. The victory was won the moment you yourself voluntarily began to *will* to be converted.

From that moment it was easier for God to work in you. From then on, you were *with* Him; before you were *against* Him.

Nevertheless, you were still in His way.

Not with your *will,* for you had now willed to become converted. But with your *ignorance.* All you had as yet was the Old Adam's view of conversion. And that view is wrong from first to last.

For that reason God had to continue to work in you, in order to make you understand what conversion is.

You thought that to be converted meant to decide by your own will power to cease your former manner of life, to remove your desire toward sin, and to compel yourself to love God by the combined powers of your own will.

But now God has worked in you, and you know from your own experience that it is impossible for you to do these things. Your "mouth has been stopped," and you yourself brought "under the judgment of God." You know now that in you, that is, in your flesh, dwelleth no good thing.

God would now show you that conversion is not a decision on your part by which you can *change* your own will, but a decision by which you declare that you are in agreement with God when He says that your will has been completely ruined by sin and is absolutely useless in this respect. Whereby you also declare yourself in agreement with God when He says that your only hope is to have God create a new will within you, in fact, a whole new being.

Hear the gospel of conversion: This new thing *God* will work in you. Because you cannot. All you have to do is to declare yourself in agreement with God when He says that your old will is impotent. When you now by the light and guidance of the Spirit experience how impotent and how evil your own will is, do not despair or lose courage; simply go to God and say, "Dear Lord, Thou seest how useless my own will is. Create within me a new will. And after Thou hast created it, continue Thou to strengthen this new will within me."

By this time you no doubt understand that you should not try in your own strength to change the situation in which you find yourself every time a desire toward sin manifests itself within you, every time you feel that you are worldly and a stranger to God, with no desire to read the Word of God and to pray, and every time you feel that you find but little joy in doing the will of God.

Instead you should acknowledge the facts as they are, and that at once. Then God will do what God alone can do: He will *forgive* you.

This does not seem plausible or possible to you. And in this you are right. To forgive sinners is such a serious matter with God that He Himself had to become incarnate and give His blood for us in order to forgive us our sins.

But when God has forgiven you, then the new-created will which He gave to you when you were born anew is strengthened. Then He can once more freely and unhindered work in your will in such a way that you both will and work in conformity with the will of God.

Is not this a beautiful text?

Only strange that practically no one ever preaches on it to us. It contains an especially inspiring gospel, because it shows us conversion in its full evangelical light.

As a rule conversion is preached to us in such a way that we see it only as a *requirement*.

Which is as it should be, of course, because conversion is a requirement also.

But it is first and foremost a *gift*.

Philippians 2:12 is, however, really written to believing Christians.

The passage contains some deep thoughts, thoughts which at first glance appear to be self-contradictory.

Let us consider them briefly.

It says, "*Work* out your own salvation."

Can this be reconciled with the plain words of the Scriptures about salvation being by grace, apart from works, that is, without work? Ephesians 2:8-9; Romans 4:5; 3:20.

Especially striking is the fact that it is *Paul* who speaks these words about working out our own salvation. He, it will be remembered, is also the one who most strongly emphasizes the unmerited aspect of salvation.

The words which follow are even more remarkable: "with fear and trembling."

Was it not Paul himself who said that "Ye received not the spirit of bondage again unto fear; but ye received the spirit of adoption, whereby we cry, Abba, Father!" (Romans 8:15)?

Which John confirms when he says, "Perfect love casteth out fear" (1 John 4:18).

Here we see how careful we must be when we read the Bible. Truth has many sides. Life is rich. Let us be careful to take into account everything that the Scriptures contain on each particular subject.

Now let us try to reconcile these statements.

In the first place, the Scriptures tell us that there is a fear which the Spirit of God casts out of a sinner's heart as soon as He has convinced him of sin and endued him with the righteousness of Christ, as soon as He can bear testimony with the sinner's spirit that he is a child of God, and has shed abroad the love of God in his heart.

The spirit of bondage vanishes, that spirit which always fears, because it knows and expects no other love and favor of God than what it has itself merited by its own fulfilment of the law.

This fear is cast out when we see that God loves us, not because we love and serve Him, but because He loves us. He loved us while we were still His enemies, and He justifies the ungodly for Christ's sake.

The spirit of bondage gives way to that childlike trust which looks confidently and with boldness up to our holy God and says, "Father!"

At the same time the Scriptures also say that there is a fear which a sinner is not saved *from* but saved *into*.

In our books of catechetical instruction this fear is called childlike fear, to distinguish it from that which we have just mentioned, which is called slavish fear.

The expression *childlike* fear is a good one because this fear is characteristic of the children, the sons, of God.

In Luke 12:4 and following verses Jesus speaks to His friends about this fear.

First, He tells them of the various kinds of fear which they should overcome. Then He mentions one fear which they should retain:

"But I will warn you whom ye shall fear: Fear him, who after he hath killed hath power to cast into hell; yea, I say unto you, *Fear him.*"

Here, Jesus says, is a fear of God which has a place in discipleship, in sonship. There is a connection, Jesus says, between this fear and the fact that God is a consuming fire toward all sin to such a degree that He casts that sinner into hell with both body and soul who definitely refuses to let God save him from his sins.

Here it appears as if childlike fear is exactly like slavish fear, because the spirit of bondage is also afraid of the punishment of God, and, naturally, of hell especially.

But here, too, we see, upon closer examination, the great difference between these two kinds of fear.

Slavish fear is the kind which is afraid of the punishment only. It looks upon God as a harsh, strict, and despotic Lord, who really would rather punish than do anything else.

Childlike fear, on the other hand, is not afraid of the punishment only, but of sin itself, of the very idea of sinning against God, of violating the will of God, of grieving His heart.

For this reason some have wanted to define childlike fear as *reverence*. Which is right enough; childlike fear includes everything that we mean by reverence, from holy respect to blind submission.

But if childlike fear is defined *only* as reverence, then it is limited in a way which is incompatible with the words of Jesus and Paul quoted above. "Fear and trembling," Paul says. Both these expressions connote more than reverence or awe. When Jesus tells His disciples to fear the God who casts into hell, it is clear that He uses the word fear in its most direct sense, namely, a lively feeling that God is one who is *dangerous*.

Right here is the fundamental difference between fear and reverence. The feelings connoted by reverence are of various hues, none of which suggest anything dangerous in connection with the one reverenced.

But the feeling which we call fear suggests at once something dangerous. And when Jesus says that we should *fear* God, He thereby says that there is something *dangerous* about God.

And no man can escape feeling that there is something dangerous about God, provided he comes close enough to Him.

But we must remember that we human beings have misunderstood every aspect of God—including the dangerous aspect.

We notice that in Israel it was looked upon as dangerous to *see* God, that is, receive a revelation of God. That meant death. In Judges 13:22 we read, "And Manoah said unto his wife, We shall surely die, because we have seen God." See also Judges 6:22. This was, of course, a misunderstanding, as the account itself clearly shows.

But God desired to impress upon His chosen people that there *was* something dangerous about God; wherefore they should fear Him.

Through His revelation of Himself He taught them that the dangerous aspect of God was connected with His holiness, that is, His hatred of sin.

That is why God is dangerous to sinners. Not to all sinners, however. God is not a God whom humble, repentant, and confessing sinners need fear, because they have availed themselves of the grace made possible to them by the sacrifice of the New Covenant and thus have received atonement for their sins. He is now their merciful and loving Savior, who delivers them out of all danger.

But God is dangerous to those sinners who disobey His commandments and set at naught Christ's sacrificial atonement. Think of Nadab and Abihu, who offered strange fire before Jehovah. They were devoured on the spot by fire (Exodus 10:1-2). Or think of Korah, Dathan, and Abiram who stirred up rebellion against Moses and Aaron and were swallowed up by the earth in the very presence of the people (Leviticus 16:1-35).

In the Old Covenant this dangerous aspect of God was given *outward* expression. We might think of what is told about Uzzah in 2 Samuel 6:6-9. The Old Covenant was temporary and preparatory, which accounts for such outward manifestations.

In the New Covenant we no longer have this. In it we have the full light of revelation also with respect to the *dangerous aspect* of God. Jesus touches upon it in the passage from Luke 12 cited above.

He says that the dangerous thing about God is His holiness, which casts both body and soul into hell if the sinner despises and rejects His salvation. Jesus would have His disciples know and feel this danger in connection with God.

Moreover, this fear is a childlike fear and arises from a different source than slavish fear. It cannot be experienced except by those who have accepted the grace of God and who know the love of God. This fear proceeds naturally from our knowledge of God whose love is so great that He cannot tolerate sin, and therefore must cast us into hell if we misuse His saving grace.

We notice, too, that Jesus did not only speak about this fear. He Himself felt it in His own sinless soul. Jesus was afraid of only one thing, but that He feared above all else: to misuse His Father's love.

Jesus gave expression to this fear in various ways.

Thus in His sharp words to His mother, "Woman, what have I to do with thee?" (John 2:4). No doubt He felt at the time that her prayer was a temptation to Him to act before the Father's appointed hour.

Or His words to Peter, "Get thee behind me, Satan" (Matthew 16:23).

Or when the Greeks came to see Jesus: "Now is my soul troubled; and what shall I say?" (John 12:27). But above all, of course, we think of His anxiety of soul in Gethsemane and on the cross.

The deepest element in Jesus' fear in connection with His passion was without question His fear of the diabolical temptations which at that time were crowding in upon His lonely soul. At that time He felt the temptation to disobedience more than at any other time.

His *fear* of these temptations was undoubtedly the human expression of God's own eternal *hatred* of sin.

The childlike fear which we have resembles this.

Because we are born of God and have been made partakers of divine nature, we have also been made partakers of God's holy hatred and fear of sin. And this manifests itself in a conscientious child of God, as in Jesus, in anxiety of soul lest he sin, lest he act contrary to the will of God.

The childlike aspect of this fear is seen most clearly in the fact that it is sin which is feared, not merely the consequences of sin, sin as that which makes separation between us and God, casts us away from God, and, if we continue therein, casts us with body and soul into hell.

The childlike aspect of this fear reveals itself also in the fact that it does not decrease but rather increases in the believing soul as time passes. Never is it stronger than when a believer lives a fresh and rich life in God. The more he lives by grace and the more he learns to know grace in all its forgiving and transforming power, the more he feels the *risk connected with grace*.

Unquestionably this is what Paul had in mind when he wrote the words, "Work out your own salvation with fear and trembling; for it is God who worketh in you both to will and to work." The fact that God does all from first to last is what produces our deepest fears.

*

In his explanation of the commandments, Luther begins every one with these words, "We should fear and love God and . . . ."

It is perhaps well known that there are some Christians today who maintain that Luther made a mistake in this. They strike out the "fear" and say that we should love God, nothing more.

But when the people of our superficial generation have read the Bible as thoroughly as Luther did, they will see that Luther was right also in this.

He has seen clearly that love to God does not exclude fear, but that they mutually strengthen each other.

He has seen that there is something about love which is to be feared. He has seen that there is something about grace which is dangerous. He has seen the risk connected with grace, yea, that in the last instance nothing is more dangerous than the grace of God.

It is part and parcel of the risk connected with life as a whole.

The greater the good in life, the more dangerous it becomes to us, *if we misuse it.* And since the grace of God is life's most precious good, grace is more dangerous than anything else in the world, if we misuse it.

The psalmist saw this more than two thousand years ago when he said, "Blessed is the man unto whom the Lord imputeth not iniquity, *and in whose spirit there is no guile"* (Psalm 32:2).

This is the precipitous chasm which runs along the narrow way to the very end—to our dying breath. As long as a Christian is watchful and keeps his eye on this chasm, he will continue to live in "fear and trembling," as the apostle admonishes us to do.

*

"Work out your own salvation . . . for it is God who worketh in you both to will and to do."

These words, too, sound mutually self-contradictory to those who have had no *experience* in the matter.

To the Christian believer, however, these words are a profound and beautiful description of some of his most blessed experiences.

He knows that it is God who worketh in him. And that from first to last He can with a whole heart say with Paul, "All things are of God."

Everything is of God: creation, redemption, baptism, the call, repentance, faith, regeneration, and sanctification.

Everything that has taken place within him has been wrought by God. Also that which has taken place in his will, that which he himself of his own will has freely chosen and decided upon. This is the blessed mystery of life in God, that God works in our wills and gradually overcomes their opposition until we ourselves, freely and of our own accord, will and choose the things which are in harmony with God's will.

Our *salvation* takes place in the same way. We are daily under the power of the creating and transforming will of God, and we *lose* our souls when we *withdraw* ourselves from this transforming influence of the will of God (Hebrews 10:38-39).

This throws light upon the words of the apostle, "Work . . . it is God who worketh in you."

There *is* a work, then, for us to do in the matter of our souls' salvation.

And this work consists of this one thing: Not to withdraw ourselves from the transforming power of God's will as it works in our wills. Our work consists in seeing to it that we day by day are receptive to the influence and the workings of God in our lives.

We are to see to it that neither carelessness nor diligence, neither earthly-mindedness nor preoccupation with our own affairs, neither pride nor discouragement, neither toil nor ease cut us off from a steady supply of divine power.

One who is to take a radium treatment also has something very definite to do, namely, to see to it that the affected part of his body is in the proper proximity to the radium, and that nothing disturbs the healing action of the radium. It is the radium, however, which effects the cure, not the concern, the effort, the thoughts, the feelings, or the exertion of the patient.

Oh, if we could only learn this also when it is a question of the strongest of all healing powers: the will of God!

*

Now, God works in us through *means*.

Especially through the means of grace, the Word and the Sacraments. Our work, therefore, is to make constant use of these means, that is, to give God the necessary time and opportunity to reach us with the saving, life-giving, and sanctifying powers of His will.

We will make use of the means of grace in an entirely different way when we begin to look upon them in this light.

The idea is not that I am to present something meritorious to God by means of my Bible reading, my attendance at the communion table, my prayers, or my participation in the communion of saints; rather it is the power of God's grace which is to accomplish something within me, through these means.

Using the means of grace *in this way* will afford us quietude of soul during our devotional exercises, which in turn will afford us seasons of rest and refreshing such as we hitherto have never known.

Also when striving against our sins, it is God who works in us both to will and to do. Our work consists in *not withdrawing* ourselves from the light of God, not concealing or excusing our sins. Every time we *confess* our sins, Christ gains unhindered access to work in us, first forgiveness and then deliverance. This deliverance takes place, as we know, step by step throughout our whole earthly life. Oftentimes we can see no progress, but nevertheless we are little by little set free from our inner sinfulness every time we make a sincere confession of defeat. That gives Christ access to our wills again.

Also when it is a question of serving the Lord, it is God who works in us. Our work in this connection is to permit ourselves to be *led* by the Spirit and *constrained* by the love of Christ (Romans 8:14; 2 Corinthians 5:14).

Then we experience what the apostle meant when he wrote, "We are his workmanship, created in Christ Jesus for good works, which God afore prepared that we should walk in them."

This imparts to our service in the Kingdom of God a peculiar sense of calmness and security. It saves us from busybodiness and from love of display, and teaches us that it is not so much a question of *what* we do as *how* we do it.

It also places upon us a sacred responsibility. God wills to work through us. He wills to transmit His wonder-working powers through us to those about us. We must not, therefore, permit the connection between us and God to be severed, in order that we may be channels for the uninterrupted flow of power from above.

*

Paul says to Timothy: "Exercise thyself unto godliness."

If you, my dear reader, have exercised yourself unto godliness as little as I have, then let us begin at once in earnest thus to exercise ourselves!

And let us begin by following the directions given by our Lord:

"Every one that asketh, receiveth."

Faith and Assurance

*"If we confess our sins, he is faithful and righteous
to forgive us our sins, and to cleanse us from all
unrighteousness."*

—1 John 1:9.

MY purpose in writing what I am about to write
is to help seeking, sorrowing, and inquiring
souls. What they look like from the outside,
I do not know. But I do know a little about
how they look on the inside. And by way of introduction
I would like to dwell upon this briefly, in order that they
might the more easily recognize themselves.

Permit me to mention the following four lines which I
see upon their inner faces.

1. *They have chosen.*

They no longer face both ways and try to be somewhat
religious when the occasion demands it and somewhat
worldly when *that* suits the occasion better.

They have chosen to share ill treatment with the people
of God. Which in itself is a great joy. You who have
chosen, lay this book aside for a while and thank God
from the depths of your soul that you have entered in
through the narrow gate of decision.

2. *They are people in whose hearts there is no guile.*

They have a holy suspicion of themselves. They are
always afraid lest deception and trickery find a place in
their hearts and lives. If they could, they would gladly
turn their hearts inside out in order to make absolutely

certain that they were hiding nothing, that they were not trying to smuggle a single sin into their spiritual life.

3. *They have begun right in their Christian lives.*

They began by taking up immediately the battle against the sinful habits which they had been practising day after day in their home life. And that is all we have to do in order to learn to know what it means to be anxious because of sin. They see every day that they do not love God; they see that they love themselves above all else. Moreover, they feel that they have no regret or remorse, that their hearts are in fact as cold as ice and as hard as stone.

4. *They read the Bible.*

They read it every day, whether they have a desire to do so or not.

And in the Bible they read that God is gracious, in fact, that His greatest joy is to save sinners.

*

But some one will no doubt ask immediately:

"Do you mean to say that such people as these are seeking, sorrowing, inquiring souls? It seems to me that they must be Christians who have been made happy in the Lord and whom the Son has made free indeed, if they are what you have described in the preceding!"

Naturally, some of them are that.

But not all. Strangely enough!

If you ask them why they are not, you will receive an answer at once.

And it will be, "If I could only *believe.*"

"But since I cannot believe, what good does the grace of God do me?"

A remarkable situation, indeed!

*

When God laid out the way of salvation for sinful man, He had to make it as *simple* as possible. Therefore

He appointed the way of *faith*. Sinners are saved through faith. Otherwise none of us would reach glory.

But we have bungled this matter so badly that seeking souls scarcely know of anything more difficult than to believe.

This is strange.

On the one hand we have the sinner, who knows of nothing that he would rather do than surrender himself with all his guilt to the Savior. On the other hand we have God, who knows of nothing that He would rather do than take this weary and aching soul to His own loving heart.

To think that these two cannot find each other, although they both desire most earnestly to do so! Because there is a little piece of mechanism known as faith, and until it has clicked properly God cannot help a poor soul no matter how much He would like to do so!

Certainly it is not difficult to see that there must be a misunderstanding here somewhere.

Moreover, the seeking souls of today are not alone to blame for this.

We preachers must take the greater share of the blame, because our preaching on the subject of faith is not clear and simple enough.

Do not misunderstand me. We certainly preach the best way we know how, all of us. If we could do better, we would certainly try to do so.

The thing is that while faith is something exceedingly simple, we tend to make it intricate and involved when we speak about it.

*

As I see it, preaching on the subject of faith has as a rule followed two general trends.

The preaching of the older generation emphasized strongly that faith is a gift of God, and that we receive it in God's appointed hour. To the seeking soul these preachers said, "You must *wait;* in God's appointed hour you will *receive* faith." They frequently made use of the verse:

> Wait in stillness in thy heart;
> He will peace to thee impart.

Then came a *newer* and freer type of preaching.

It asked, "Where does the Bible say that you should wait before you believe? Nowhere. On the contrary, it says, 'Believe on the Lord Jesus, and thou shalt be saved, thou and thy house!'" (Acts 16:31).

"Believe *now,* and you will *be* saved!"

And to this the preachers of this school would add, "Why do you continue to grieve Jesus by your unbelief?"

Some would even go farther and say, "You can secure forgiveness for all your other sins, for Jesus' sake; but if you do not believe, you are already condemned, because you have not believed on the name of the only begotten Son of God.

These two ways of presenting faith are, obviously, very different. They agree, however, in one respect. Both confuse faith and assurance, and present them as one and the same thing.

When the older generation of preachers said, "Wait for the appointed time of the Lord and you will receive *faith,* they meant *assurance.*

And when the preachers of a later day said, "Believe now and you will be saved," they meant: "You will receive assurance."

Thus seeking souls understood them too.

And therefore they tried with all their might to gain assurance. They followed all the well-meant advice that was given them. They tried putting their own names into Isaiah 53:5 and many other Scripture passages. But they

did not succeed. Home they had to go, with one more
stone added to the heavy load that they were already
dragging along.

*

In trying to say a few words about faith, I would like
to take as my starting point 1 John 1:9: "If we confess
our sins, he is faithful and righteous to forgive us our
sins, and to cleanse us from all unrighteousness."

To be sure, faith is not mentioned here.

But, on the other hand, this passage tells me more
clearly than any other passage in the Bible what is necessary *for me to do* in order to be saved.

This passage speaks about the forgiveness of sins, and
it must certainly be clear to everybody that whoever has
the forgiveness of sins is saved.

What must I do on my part to secure the forgiveness
of sins?

The answer is very clear: "If we confess."

Nothing more.

Simple, is it not?

But some reader, who perhaps does more thinking than
the average, will no doubt ask, "Where is faith mentioned
here? Can a man be saved without faith?"

No, one cannot; "without faith it is impossible to be
well-pleasing unto him" (Hebrews 11:6).

Consequently, it is clear that faith must be understood
in some way in the passage, "If we confess our sins, he is
faithful and righteous to forgive us our sins, and to
cleanse us from all unrighteousness."

Faith must be and is there, even if it is not mentioned.

But where is it?

This is almost a Biblical word-puzzle; but if we can
find and see faith in this verse, we have solved the
problem of faith.

Faith is in the confession.

Which is self-evident, if we will only reflect a little.

When, as far as we are concerned, only one condition is named upon which we may receive the forgiveness of sins, namely, that we confess them, and when we know from the Scriptures otherwise that no one can be saved except through faith, then we know that faith *must* be included in the confession.

This throws new light at once upon the question of faith.

To have faith is to confess your sins to the Savior.

That person has faith unto salvation who believes in the Savior to such a degree that he comes to Him and confesses his sins to Him.

Now I ask you, you who have never been able to believe, "Have you ever confessed your sins to God?"

"Yes, I have," you say. "I did that a long time ago. And I have done it a countless number of times since."

Very well; excellent! Now read the verse over again. And you will see that you *are* already saved; you *are* a child of God.

I have the right to declare unto you by the authority of God's own Word the gracious forgiveness of all your sins.

No man can *forgive* sin. Only God can do that. But men are permitted to *declare* unto each other that forgiveness which God has already granted, whenever it is difficult for any of us to apprehend the forgiveness of God.

In this case it is you who have had difficulty in believing that God has forgiven you your sins, but I see clearly that you are mistaken in this. I see that God Himself says in this passage that He has granted you forgiveness. And for that reason I have authority to declare unto you this forgiveness.

You are saved, then, even though you for the time being do not feel very much of the joy, peace, or assurance connected with salvation.

Herein is where you have misunderstood faith.

You have talked all the time about *believing yourself saved,* about believing yourself to be a child of God. The Scriptures say nothing about that. They speak only of *believing in Christ,* or, what amounts to the same thing, having faith in God.

You have thought that salvation takes place within you, and that as soon as it is accomplished you will, as a child of God, experience blessed feelings, such as, joy, peace, and assurance.

You forgot that forgiveness is an act which takes place, not *in you* but *in heaven.*

May I now make use of some figures from the Bible and describe what takes place in heaven when God forgives sin?

Down here on earth a great deal of sensation is not created as a rule when a sinner becomes convicted of sin and begins to struggle through to salvation. But in heaven this is followed with intense interest. See Luke 15:7, 10; Hebrews 12:1.

In heaven they have followed you from the time you stopped before the light which led to your spiritual awakening. They saw you turn about and begin to go in the direction of that sharp, penetrating light. The farther you went, the worse things seemed to you to become. You began to see more and more of your sins. At last you saw nothing but sin. No matter what you said or did, there was sin in it. If you failed to do certain things, *that,* too, was sin. You found as you stood before God in this blinding light that there was not even true remorse in your soul, not even a will to be saved; your heart was divided against itself.

Furthermore, you saw that you in your own strength could not alter the condition in which you found yourself.

Then what did you do?

You did what every sincere soul has resorted to in distress of this kind. You did what a man does when he falls into the water and is drowning. You cried out with all the strength that was in you. No doubt you cried out about as Peter did: "Lord, save me!"

Then it came to pass.

He came who had been following the whole process that was taking place, He who had started it, led, and guided it. Carefully He laid hold of you with His pierced hands, lifted you out of the mire, washed you, and made you white in His crimson blood.

Then He took out the book of heaven, in which your sins were written, from the greatest and foulest to the very least, and forthwith crossed them all out with His blood.

Thus He cancelled the whole charge that was against you. You were now entirely free of debt.

But He did more than that, it says. He took all your sins and cast them behind His back into the depths of the sea.

By this simple figure He would make it plain to you that He will remember your sins no more. Nor ever again remind you of them.

Then He took out the book of life, and wrote your name therein.

You had become a *child of God*. Declared by God to be such with an authority which cannot be disputed either on earth or in hell.

Furthermore, it made no difference how you felt. You were now a child of God, regardless of how you felt. Even if you did not feel anything!

For your salvation is not dependent upon your feelings,

but upon that which God, according to His unchangeable Word, does for sinners on the basis of what Christ by His suffering and death has accomplished for them.

*

However, it is not easy to comfort a conscientious soul.

A hypocrite will heap to himself aid and comfort from wherever he can find it in the whole universe.

The conscientious soul, on the other hand, is born with a holy suspicion of himself. He is always afraid of deceiving himself.

He knows that the passage of Scripture referred to is plain enough. Every one who confesses his sins, receives the forgiveness of sins.

But he asks himself, "Have I confessed? I have, it is true, spoken with God in my prayers about my sins. But is it certain that I have done what Scripture means by confessing?"

To help you, let me at this point ask you a question.

You no doubt remember the time when you as a child had done something wrong, and you stood in the presence of your father and mother, about to confess your wrong-doings. Now I ask you, "Can you remember that you were ever in doubt as to whether you had really confessed or not?"

No, you were not; you knew full well that you had truly confessed.

Why?

Because to confess was a very simple thing, only to tell truthfully exactly what you had done.

That was what your father and mother were waiting for. They were not particularly interested in how you cried and carried on. Their loving eyes were on the look-out for one thing and that only, whether the little wrong-doer was telling the whole truth. As soon as you told them everything, you well remember how happy they became. They took you to their hearts, said that the past was all forgotten, and that everything was all right again.

To confess to God is no more complicated than that. All He expects of you is that you acknowledge your sins to the full extent to which your conscience prompts you. If you have done this, you have confessed.

And the Bible says that you have the forgiveness of sins.

Thank Him for this. And do it now! Gladden His heart by your gratitude!

*

But many a conscientious soul still has fears of deceiving himself.

And asks therefore, "Have I confessed everything?"

I can well understand why you ask. You have had certain experiences since your conversion which cause you to be in doubt on this point.

You had lived for some time with God, and thought that you had confessed everything to Him. Suddenly one day—or one night perhaps—you remembered a sin, perhaps a sin against some individual, a sin for which you had not made amends. Or you caught yourself living in a sin which you before had simply not known was sin at all. So blind had you been.

You became anxious and asked yourself, "If I have overlooked such things when I have confessed, how about my confession as a whole? Perhaps the whole thing is nothing but self-deception."

Here again let me try to help you by asking you a question: "Do you know of any sin that you have committed that you have knowingly and willingly sought to conceal from God, that is, not confess?"

No doubt you will answer as so many others have answered me, "No; do you think that I would do anything like that?"

No, I did not think you would; but I wanted you to be certain about this. For he who confesses everything he knows and not knowingly or willingly seeks to hide anything from God, he makes a true confession.

That you later, as time passes, see more and more of your sinfulness, as it comes to light in your experience, is another matter.

This occurs because the Holy Spirit is continually pointing out to us our sins. We of ourselves are not capable of seeing or grieving over our sins. It is the Spirit who "convicts the world of sin," Jesus says.

During our awakening and conversion we do not see or feel sorry for any more sins than those which the Holy Spirit points out to us. In the case of most of us the Spirit acts in such a way as *not* to point out all our sins at one time. He deals with us in that way no doubt because we could not endure to see all of them at one time.

This enlightens us also as to the successive and progressive nature of what we term the knowledge of sin. We should not become anxious or bewildered because we become progressively conscious of sins which we had never been aware of before.

There is something particularly gracious in this whole arrangement. By so doing God does not deprive His children of their peace and confidence.

Precisely as we do in the case of our children.

We do not desire to see them in a state of continual fretfulness and anxiety, asking themselves if father and mother have anything against them. We want them to feel happy and free in their homes. We tell them that we will let them know if a thing is sinful or wrong, and to be on their guard themselves. We tell them that we will let them know if they do anything that is wrong, and if they do not see themselves that a thing is wrong, we will speak to them. And we tell them that when we do that, we expect them to heed us and to acknowledge their wrong-doing.

Thus our heavenly Father, too, deals with His children.

He says to you, "You who have received Christ as a gift, be happy and feel free. You do not need anything more in life or in death. Go your way, with gratitude in your heart and a song of praise upon your lips. Do your daily work hopefully and cheerfully. Sin cleaves to you and works all manner of coveting within you; but be of good cheer, and have no fears because of this. My Spirit shall warn you and keep you lest you be tempted and fall. And if you do fall, my Spirit shall speak to you about your sins until you feel sorry for them and confess them and you are again restored and forgiven."

Is not this a gracious arrangement?

*

After what we have now observed, it is comparatively easy to see that faith is not a matter of *feeling* or sentiment, as many people mistakenly take it to be.

As long as faith is looked upon essentially as a matter of feeling, there will be something capricious and moody about it. Something like a lottery. If you are lucky, you win the big prize. And if you do not win, there is nothing to do about it.

If you are lucky, you get your faith to function. If you fail to get it to work, there is nothing to do about it. So some people think.

But this is a complete misunderstanding.

Faith, like repentance, is a matter of the *will*.

This is clear from the Scriptures.

In the first place, it is clear from Scripture's *admonition* to believe:

"Believe on the Lord Jesus Christ!" . . . An admonition is always addressed to the will.

In the next place, it is clear from the fact that in the Scriptures faith is designated as "the obedience of faith" (Romans 1:5, 16:26). Whatever has to do with obedience is, of course, always a matter of the will.

Finally, this is clear also from the fact that the Scriptures characterize *unbelief* as *disobedience*. The expression which is used in the Greek New Testament to designate unbelief means in ordinary Greek disobedience.

But if unbelief is disobedience, it is clear that faith is obedience. And both, obedience and disobedience, must be a matter of the will.

*

Since faith is a matter of the will, it must involve a *decision*.

What do we mean by decision in connection with faith?

After what we have said up to this point, we can answer as follows: The decision involved is whether I will allow myself to be convicted of the Spirit and confess my sins, or whether I will *withdraw* myself from the convicting work of the Spirit, and thus from reconciliation with God.

Now I can imagine that here and there some one will be sitting and reading this book with deep inner anxiety. Already they have asked themselves: "If faith is defined as a matter of the will, do we not come in conflict with the Bible when it says that the natural man is utterly incapable of apprehending and comprehending the things of God? The thing that Luther in our catechetical books has expressed thus: "I believe that I cannot through my own reason or strength believe in Jesus Christ."

At first glance there does seem to be a contradiction here. Let us therefore consider this a little more closely.

When we say that faith is a matter of the will, we

would not thereby have it said that the natural man can by his own will believe.

Far from it.

If there is anything that the natural man cannot do of himself, it is to have faith *in God*.

He can believe in men, in animals, in money, and it almost seems as though he can also believe in the devil.

But in God?

No. Men look upon Him as a dangerous Being, and keep as far away from Him as they possibly dare.

No miracle is so incomprehensibly great as the one by which God persuades a hostile and rebellious human heart to believe in Him.

This He does through the new-creating miracle which we call awakening, in which God calls a man in such a way that he feels attracted to the living God and is brought face to face with His all-seeing eyes.

This done, God proceeds to speak to this man who has spent his past life in levity. He speaks to him about his sins and about the salvation which He has accomplished, and tells him that He is willing to save also him.

Now comes the decision of faith.

The sinner must *choose,* either to flee from God, and thus to flee from reconciliation with Him, or, if he decides to be obedient to the heavenly vision, to confess his sins.

This decision is the decision of *faith.*

That is, here is a decision which must be made in faith, a decision which proceeds from faith. This decision is solely one of faith, wholly and entirely an act of daring, based upon faith. See what is said about this above, on page 41.

The old Haugean Christians of Norway had a perfectly brilliant way of expressing this. They said, "To believe is to come to Christ with your sins."

It is scarcely possible to express this more briefly, more simply, and more profoundly than they have done it.

Here we have all the elements which constitute faith. Faith is faith in *Christ*. And faith is the sinner's fleeing to Christ with all his *sins*. And faith is a matter of the *will*. Faith is nothing else than the will to come to Christ with our every sin.

*

Because salvation is by grace *this* faith is sufficient unto salvation for any sinner.

It is Christ who saves the sinner.

And the sinner does not have to assist Christ in the work of salvation. Christ does not need any *assistance*. All He needs is *access*. And this He gains by faith. When the sinner comes to Christ with his sins, Christ gains access to him with His powers of salvation, and saves him.

Permit me to explain this aspect of faith by means of an illustration.

Let us suppose that you became ill.

It developed into a protracted siege, and finally your doctor advised you to consult a specialist. You did. And the specialist took a great deal of time and examined you thoroughly. When at last he had finished, his face wore a serious look. Finally he said:

"This is a very serious case, and I am not certain that we can treat you successfully. In order to succed at all, you must submit to an operation, and I must tell you beforehand that it will be a very dangerous one. Moreover, I cannot say what the outcome will be."

Now I ask you, what must you do on your part in order to be operated upon?

Pardon me for asking such foolish questions. But what I want to do is to lead your mind away from the usual misconceptions concerning faith.

Once again, then, what does the surgeon expect of you before he can operate upon you? Does he expect you to be absolutely calm and certain that the outcome will be successful? So you can comfort him and say, "Dear doctor, you must not take it so seriously; everything will go all right"?

No, of course not.

Or do you think he expects you to sit there happy and pleased over the fact that you are to be operated upon?

No, not that either, of course.

He does not expect anything but what he is accustomed to seeing: a sick, worried, perhaps despairing, human being, who sits speechless while great tears trickle down your pallid cheeks.

But there is *something* that he does expect of you; and unless you do it he cannot operate.

And that is not much. He can manage very nicely even though all you can say is: "Will you be kind enough to try, doctor!"

That is what he needs from your side, namely, confidence in him, so that you will entrust your body with all its ills to him.

And note this: you *will be* operated upon. *He* will do the operating. You will be present only objectively.

You are not to help him.

On the contrary, he will see to it that you do not interfere and disturb him in the least while he is operating. You will be given an anesthetic and be completely removed from the scene. Only your body will be present.

To make certain that you in your unconscious state do not become restless and disturb him, he will have you bound hand and foot.

Not until then can he begin to operate.

We will take it for granted that the operation is

Under His Wings

successful. It is on the whole phenomenal what some of our skilful and conscientious surgeons can do.

The operation over, the mask is removed from your face; and they wheel you into the room you are to have. In a little while you gradually begin to come to. When the surgeon is through in the operating room, he steps into your room for a moment. He looks pleased and says, "Just be as quiet as you can; you are going to be well again."

Well, it is easy enough to be quiet, for the simple reason that you cannot move. But well again? Impossible! You were sick before, but you are much worse now than ever.

The next day the doctor comes again and says, "Everything is coming along fine."

Oh, is that so! It was bad yesterday; but today it is even worse after a terrible night. The large incision has now begun to pain and weaken you.

The next day the great surgeon comes again, and repeats that everything is coming along nicely.

Well, by this time you, too, have to admit that you are feeling a *little* better.

And after from eight to fourteen days have elapsed, you agree entirely with the doctor. Your life has been saved. He knew it at once, but you were not certain of it until after the pains had begun to leave you, and you knew from that that the cause of your illness had been removed.

*

You undoubtedly know what I am driving at. The similarity between this and the salvation of a soul is very striking.

Our souls, too, are sick. Sick unto death.

They can be saved only by a major operation.

And there is only one surgeon who can perform it, the healer of souls, Jesus Christ.

And He really can do it, too. He has never been unsuccessful in a single operation.

Now what is necessary for us to do on our part in order to be operated upon by Him?

First, to realize that we are sick. Next, to come to Him with our sins.

That is all He expects of us.

Many people think they must first be happy and have peace and assurance. If they do not have that, they think that they cannot be children of God.

This is to invert the order of things. It is right for you to look forward to peace and assurance, and eventually you *will* become happy and experience full assurance.

But this is not the beginning.

The beginning is *painful,* because it begins with an operation. This Jesus performs. And He performs it the moment we believe.

From our side all He expects is faith, that is, that we have confidence in Him and come to Him with our soul's diseases, not concealing any of our sins from Him, and leave ourselves to His care, in the same way as a patient leaves himself in a doctor's care.

Christ knows about the pains which follow upon an operation of this kind, and is therefore not surprised if we do not have very much joy, peace, or assurance while the conversion-operation is taking place.

Nor should you allow yourself to become bewildered because of the soul-pain, the anxiety of heart, which you are now experiencing. The dissatisfaction with yourself, the despising, even loathing, of yourself, the despair over the boundless sinfulness of your heart, over its callousness and lack of feelings, over the half-heartedness of your will, and the vacillation which you are now experi-

encing are merely *pains resulting from the operation.*
Christ cannot lance the carbuncles of sin without hurting.

But be of good cheer! These pains are not dangerous.
They are signs of *life* and not of *death,* just as birth-
pains are.

*

From the ideas that we have developed thus far, it is
apparent that we have borne in mind all the time the
distinction between *faith* and *assurance.*

We have tried to bring out the consolation there is in
the fact that we are saved by faith and not by assurance.
And that faith is nothing else than to come to Christ with
our sins.

But now I can imagine some one asking, "Are not faith
and assurance the same thing? Is it possible to distinguish
between them? Does not Hebrews 11:1 say, 'Faith is
assurance of things hoped for'?"

To this I would answer first: "Yes, if we wish to state
what faith is in its fully developed form—as the author of
Hebrews does—then we must say without equivocation:
faith is assurance. All sound and normal faith should
develop into assurance.

We do exactly the same thing when we speak of man.
We speak of a full-grown, fully developed man.

It does not occur to anyone on that account to deny that
this fully developed man *began* life as a child. Nor does
any one deny that he was a human being when he was
only a child. But, of course, he was not as yet a fully
developed human being.

The clearest passages concerning faith and assurance
which I have found in the Bible are the following three:
Romans 8:16; Galatians 4:6 and 3:26.

In Romans 8:16 we are told how a sinner receives
assurance that he is a child of God. The Spirit of God

bears witness with our spirit, that we are children of God. Clearly this is a firm and a glorious assurance.

In Galatians 4:6 we learn that we do not receive this Spirit and with it the testimony of the Spirit, that is, assurance, until after we have become children of God. This is plain from the passage itself: *"Because* ye are sons, God sent forth the Spirit of his Son into our hearts, crying, Abba, Father."

If we do not become children of God by assurance, by the testimony of the Spirit, how then do we become His children?

This we are told in the third passage, Galatians 3:26: "For ye are all sons of God, *through faith,* in Christ Jesus."

We have received light on the relationship between faith and assurance.

Faith is the *condition* upon which we are saved.

Assurance, on the other hand, is a *fruit* and *consequence* of salvation.

*

At the same time, however, let us note that assurance is the assurance of *faith.*

There is an inner, organic connection between faith and assurance, just as there is an organic connection between the seed and the fully developed plant.

Faith begins as a tiny seed in the sinner's heart, as sorrow, anxiety, and longing, as a state in which we can no longer endure to live in sin and which therefore gives us boldness to come to Christ with every sin.

At first faith consists, as a rule, of sorrowing, sighing, questioning, doubting, groping, weeping. Most of all it doubts itself and its own existence.

But if the Spirit is permitted to continue the good work which He has begun, the operation will lead to a cure, the wounds will heal. The soul will become acquainted with the Word of God, and begin to see what it possesses in the gift which it has received, namely, God's own Son.

Restlessness and sorrow in connection with faith will disappear. The assurance of faith will develop. That is, faith will begin to see that salvation is for those who were *lost,* that God justifies the *ungodly.* Faith now becomes a rejoicing and a secure faith.

It has now reached its mature form: full assurance.

You who have come to Christ with your sins but have not as yet received assurance and found happiness, you will no doubt ask me what you should do in order to receive assurance.

Let me tell you first what you should *not* do.

Do not do as you hitherto have done perhaps. Do not seek assurance as if in a panic. Many do that, because they do not think that they are saved until they have received assurance.

It is right, however, to seek assurance. In doing so you should pray for it, as you pray for everything else that you need and that God has promised to give you.

But pray without fear. God *will* give you assurance.

And remember that it is the Spirit who works assurance, as it is He also who works faith. There is nothing that pleases Him more than to continue to explain Christ to you until you gain full assurance and are made happy in faith.

However, the Spirit works through *means.*

Use the means of grace, therefore. And when you read the Word of God, pray that the Spirit may use the Word to prepare you for the moment when He can give you assurance.

And attend the Lord's Supper.

"But should I, who do not have assurance, attend the Lord's Supper?" many ask.

Yes; every one is welcome to the Lord's Supper who

comes to Christ every day with his sins, regardless of whether he has assurance or not.

The Lord would strengthen and refresh your faith also through the sacred mystery of the Lord's Supper, in order that you might grow "unto a fullgrown man, unto the measure of the stature of the fulness of Christ."

And pray.

Tell the Lord how much you are longing for assurance, how much you need it in order that you by your daily life might be able to draw men unto Christ, and not drive them away. As it is, your life is often sad, dark, and dreary; and those who associate with you day by day are therefore not attracted to Christ very much.

Tell this to the Lord. Tell Him that you need assurance, joy, and power in order to serve Him better among your fellow men.

And He will give it to you.

Some fine day—or some dark night—when you least expect it, it will come.

He will take some brief portion of the Word of God, perform a miracle with it, and make it transparent. In a flash you will see straight through this passage of God's Word into the eternal, unbounded realm of grace beyond. You will see the Cross, the Blood, the Lamb, the Wounds as you have never seen them before. And everything will be so clear to you that you will not be able to understand why you have not been able to see them before.

When you now gather with Christian friends, you will feel a desire to tell them about it. You are certain that as soon as they hear you tell about it, it will be clear to them also.

But much to your surprise you will find when you have done it that such is not the case.

In the first place it was remarkable how difficult it was for you to make clear to others the wonderful things you had experienced. And in the second place, you found that the people you spoke to remained the same as before.

Which was most certainly to have been expected, because they, too, must receive this from God themselves, in His own appointed time. They, as well as you. God has placed certain things so high that we cannot reach them ourselves. The only way we can get them is when God Himself by a miracle puts them into our hearts.

Then and only then does faith become assurance. And, in so doing, it becomes full of joy and thanksgiving.

Just as naturally as that it was a sorrowing and a sighing faith to begin with.

Martha and Mary

"Martha, Martha, thou art anxious and troubled about many things: but one thing is needful: for Mary hath chosen the good part, which shall not be taken away from her."
—LUKE 10:41-42.

AS a rule what we read about Jesus in the gospels is taken from His *public* ministry. Here we have one of the few *interior* scenes. Jesus is visiting some of His best friends, the brother and the two sisters, in Bethany. The conversation begins at once. The disciples sit listening intently. They know what a blessed sense of the divine presence and what new glimpses into the mysteries of the Kingdom of God a quiet hour like this will bring them.

Mary becomes absorbed in the conversation at once, forgets everything else, and sits down as close to Jesus as possible in order not to miss a single word.

Martha, on the other hand, thinks of her duties as a hostess, and therefore busies herself with serving.

She, too, is vitally interested in the conversation which is taking place; but she has to go back and forth, and therefore hears only a few snatches of it.

Every time she comes in and sees Mary sitting there, she becomes impatient. At last she can contain herself no longer. She goes directly to Jesus, interrupts the conversation, and asks Him to tell Mary that she must help along with the serving so they can get through as quickly as possible, and both sit down and listen to Jesus.

But Jesus did not upbraid Mary.

On the contrary, Martha herself was rebuked, mildly but firmly.

Jesus, too, had noticed what a different effect His coming into the home had had upon the two sisters. Martha, a practical and dutiful woman, had gone to work immediately. She wanted to honor her distinguished and beloved guest, and make His stay as pleasant as possible.

Mary, on the other hand, forgot everything, so absorbed did she become in Jesus' words.

And *she* made Him the most happy. He said, "Mary hath chosen the good part, which shall not be taken away from her."

To Martha, on the other hand, He said: "The thing that you are anxious about is all well and good; you certainly mean it well. But right *now* there is something that is even more important than serving and eating. Now you have a chance to sit down and listen, an opportunity which will soon be past, and which will never return again."

Whereupon He gave her an admonition the import of which extended far beyond the situation at hand, telling her that in the midst of the many things in life *one* thing is *needful,* to be still and listen when the Lord speaks.

*

There are many Martha-souls.

In every age.

And they are oftentimes judged severely. As a rule Martha fares very badly when we preach on this text.

But let us not forget that Martha was a *believing* soul.

This is very evident from her conversation with Jesus after the death of Lazarus. See John 11:20-27. And let us not forget either that what she was anxious and troubled about was to honor her Savior and make things pleasant for Him.

That is true of all earnest Martha-souls.

They are motivated by holy zeal. Nor should we forget what they accomplish. They are *practical* people, who know how to do things. They are, moreover, capable people, who get things done; and who do not merely wax enthusiastic, talk, and lay plans.

They aim to make glad the heart of the Savior; but in this they do not succeed as the Mary-souls do.

We must also remember that Mary was not a dreamer either. She had not chosen to sit at the feet of Jesus because she was shiftless or lazy.

She, too, knew how to *act*.

We see this a few weeks later when she anoints the feet of Jesus, preparatory to His passion (John 12:1-8).

This shows us that she also knew how to choose the right time to act, as she knew how to choose the right time to sit quietly at the feet of Jesus. And on this occasion she was praised just as highly for her *action* as she had been previously for her *quietude*.

The great danger confronting the Martha-souls is to become restless and taken up with outward things.

They are impelled by a desire to serve, are always active and continually occupied with something or other in the Kingdom of God. But their many interests divide and distract their attention.

The one thing needful is inadvertently pushed to one side.

Because these people are occupied with what is, after all, Christian work, they do not seem to think that it is very dangerous to be a little neglectful of the quiet hours at the feet of Jesus.

*

From the fact that Jesus upbraided Martha as sharply as He did, even though she had a good purpose in mind with the things she was doing, it is clear that He saw here a grave danger. He would have her perceive this at once, even though the rebuke was so harsh that she perhaps felt at the time that it was both humiliating and unjust.

Without question we are here touching on a point which is fraught with great seriousness and danger to most of us. It might well be that we, too, would hear some sharp words from the lips of Jesus if we would only be still enough, so that we could hear Him speak to us.

The more experience we have had in living with the Lord and in struggling against sin, the more clear it becomes to us that there is one, and only one, temptation which is fraught with more danger than all others put together. It is the temptation to *neglect to have quiet seasons with the Lord each day.*

The danger in connection with this temptation is two-fold.

In the first place, quiet seasons at the feet of Jesus are of fundamental importance in connection with our life in God and our battle against temptation. To neglect such seasons has a weakening effect upon our whole Christian life.

In the second place, tremendous forces are at work to prevent us from having such quiet seasons, or at least to disturb us in them as much as possible.

Let us consider the latter first.

We all have an Old Adam. And there is nothing that makes Old Adam shake so much with fear as the quiet hours we have with the Lord.

He can stand a great deal of religiosity, such as religious exercises and religious work. In fact, he has no objections to prayer either, provided he does not have to risk meeting God. As we all know, he can even pray long prayers himself, provided he can gain some advan-

tage by so doing, and, above all, provided he can be certain
that it will not become so still that God's voice can be
heard.

He feels that quiet hours in the presence of the Lord
are death to him, and therefore seeks instinctively to
avoid them.

It is written: "The mind of the flesh is *enmity against
God*" (Romans 8:7). The flesh will, therefore, not object to religiosity, but it will be ever on the warpath
against God.

The flesh with its enmity against God seldom, however,
proceeds to a *direct* attack, either when opposing God or
seeking to prevent the soul from having its seasons of
quietude with Him. On the contrary, it employs *indirect*
tactics for this purpose. Which makes the attack more
dangerous.

Old Adam seldom says outright that we should neglect to have quiet seasons with the Lord. Instead, he
presents an array of most convincing arguments, either
that it is impossible for us to have such seasons or that
it is not absolutely necessary for us to have such moments
in His presence.

The number of arguments which he can present is almost endless.

And they vary in a most clever way, according to the
outward circumstances of our lives, as well as our inward
spiritual states.

In the *mornings* there is too little time, work is too
pressing.

By *noon* our souls are already filled to the brim with
the cares which attend the many activities of the day.

And in the *evening* we are tired out after the physical
and mental strain of the day.

In other words, there are more than enough reasons
why our devotional periods at any or all of these times

should be as brief as possible, according to Old Adam.

Many accept these reasons, too, as sufficient for discontinuing the quiet hour altogether.

The *devil* also concentrates all his efforts upon preventing us from keeping the quiet hour. He knows what these hours mean to us. He knows that he who daily observes the quiet hour at the feet of Jesus is invincible. The soul receives something in that hour against which the attacks of Satan are futile.

Such a soul may momentarily be led astray and transgress the will of God; but he flees at once back into the open arms of Jesus, and comes out again stronger than ever.

Satan knows that no Christian can be overcome more easily than the one who neglects to hold rendezvous with his Lord.

A human heart cannot be a void. If it is not filled with God every day, it will, nilly-willy, be filled with the world. It will follow the spiritual law of gravity and sink down, either into open or into secret worldliness. The latter is without question the most general, at least the most dangerous.

Such a heart becomes a stranger to God. Self-examination ceases. Conscience asserts itself now and then, but never so as to lead to a complete reconciliation with God. Such a soul is bleeding to death; its life is gradually ebbing out.

If the neglect of the quiet hour leads to such fatal results, is it strange that Satan concentrates all his efforts along this line?

Even though he does not succeed in disrupting completely the soul's intimate fellowship with God, only to have *weakened* our quiet hours with the Lord means a great victory for him.

The less of God's grace we receive into our souls each

day, the weaker our spiritual lives become. We wage warfare against our former manner of life with less earnestness and less determination to conquer; we content ourselves with a weak defensive, and take good care to avoid only the blameworthy and undesirable consequences of sin.

A slothful and unwilling spirit descends upon us and paralyzes our spiritual life. Our zeal for souls, for the brethren, and for God's cause as a whole becomes so weak that it scarcely manifests itself, except when renewed a little by the zeal of others.

Nor do we have very much willingness to *sacrifice,* either time, effort, or money.

Anything like crusading, conquering faith and intercession is no longer present.

And where confidence in God decreases, faith in men and in human devices increases. Soon the latter tend to occupy all our time and attention. In turn this becomes an added reason for neglecting to spend time upon our knees with our Bibles.

*

Take time for prayer!

We do not *get* time to pray; we must *take* it.

Especially important is it to take time in the morning. No matter what the cost may be, we must see to it that we never go out into the turmoil of life a single day without having had a quiet season with the Lord.

Get up early enough every morning to have time for Bible reading and prayer.

If you feel that you will get too little sleep and too little rest if you do that, then let me give you a practical little bit of advice. Go to bed earlier. Many procrastinate all evening and never get to bed. Naturally they have to make up for it in the morning. But that is not the way the Creator has ordained that it should be. The doctors can tell you that if you do not know it already.

Go to bed in the evening and sleep the sleep of the just, and you will be able to get up in the morning, refreshed and rested, with plenty of time for a quiet hour with the Lord.

Many people spoil their days, and thereby their whole lives—life consists of days,—by beginning them entirely wrong.

In the first place, they stay in bed too long in the morning.

As a result they are in a hurry, in a rush, all the time. After a grouchy morning toilet, they gulp down their breakfast and rush nervously and breathlessly off to work.

Those who begin the day in that way should not be surprised if they have a bad day and are nervous from morning till night. Nor should they be surprised if they are compelled to consult a nerve specialist after a few years.

How different the day becomes if we rise in good season, take our time dressing, have ample time for Bible reading and prayer, eat a cozy and unhurried breakfast with the family—breakfast is the most important meal of the day—and then go to work, without being in a rush or being afraid of getting to work too late.

Most people do not realize to what an extent the way we begin the day affects our attitude throughout the whole day, and thereby affects also our whole life and work. He, therefore, has learned not a little of the holy art of living who has learned to *begin* the day right.

*

Nor is the battle over when we have entered into our secret chamber. No sooner have we entered in than we are confronted with another struggle. No sooner have

we bent the knee in prayer than it seems that everything
has entered into a sworn compact to prevent us from
concentrating our thoughts. From all sides come flutter-
ing all sorts of useless and irrelevant ideas. We do not
even know where they come from. It seems as though
they are attracted to us by a magnet of some kind.

And after we have chased these thoughts away, the
useful ones present themselves for our consideration. We
begin to think of all we have to do during the day. The
one thing after the other. There are so many things!
We begin to lay out a program for the day's work. And
the more we think of all the work we have to do, the
more we feel that our time is limited. In fact, we begin
to feel that we are wasting valuable time by praying.
And then, well—then we pray as briefly as possible!

Do you see how easy it is for the enemy of our souls
to overtake us by his cunning even after we have entered
into our prayer room and closed the door? He not only
succeeds in shortening our prayer hour, but also in spoil-
ing it completely, by scattering our thoughts and making
us restless.

Verily, the battle to keep our quiet hours with the Lord
is a decisive one.

The strength of the Mary-souls is that they are fully
aware of this. They may be inferior to the Marthas in
many ways, but they have learned to guard the quiet hour
both against Satan and their own sinful flesh. And in
doing so they have chosen the *good part*.

They say with Asaph, "It is good for me to draw *near*
unto God" (Psalm 73:28).

In God's nearness they behold the glories of the eternal
realm. They hear the voice of Jesus. He speaks to
them about their sins in such a way that they weep and
shudder. But He never finishes speaking without show-
ing them His wounds and His stripes.

He thus creates a spiritual hunger and thirst in their famished hearts. And He who dwells with him that is of a contrite heart and a humble spirit, will revive the spirit of the humble and the heart of the contrite.

Their inward eyes are ever turned to the Cross; they see the Lamb of God. The Spirit explains Christ to them in such a way that they experience a remarkable, unspeakable *rest*. In spite of their wickedness of heart and their sinfulness, they build their house of salvation upon the Chief Corner-Stone. They feel as though they are borne up upon invisible arms.

In His nearness they are well protected from temptation and danger. They hear a quiet, admonishing voice which helps them when they are weakest. For they are weak, and often feel ashamed. That they get along as well as they do, they certainly do not attribute to any merit of their own. By no means; it is His preserving and keeping grace which, unmerited on their part, keeps them from suffering defeat and from falling into sin.

His love and care overwhelm them. They become bound to Him in a way that they cannot adequately describe to others. Everything in their lives is bound up with Him and centers about Him. They share everything with Him, even the most insignificant things in their daily lives. And it is this which makes their daily lives so rich, so interesting.

The quietness and the richness of their inner lives give them a poise and a balance which enable them to live through the hurry and bustle of the day unharmed. They are accustomed to share everything with the Lord. Therefore they take everything to Him. Furthermore, they are accustomed to guard the quiet *hour*. Therefore they never allow themselves to become hypnotized by the bustle of the day, but do as Luther did: If they are real busy, they pray longer than usual. They go even farther; no matter how busy they are, they do their work *together with* the Lord. In the midst of even their busiest hours their souls hold unbroken communion with Him.

Here we touch upon the great secret in the life of the Mary-souls.

They have learned to keep *near* unto God. And God is such that we need but be in His nearness in order to experience the power which emanates from Him to us, and which makes us strong in life in every way.

Their great *ability to live life* is the strength of the Mary-souls.

We have now considered briefly what such souls *receive,* namely, the good part.

But included in this good part is also the joy they experience in *giving.* They give incessantly, without knowing it themselves. They are indeed a sweet savor of Christ in every place.

Thus Mary could do more than sit still at the feet of Jesus. She could also *act* when the time came. And when she did do something, she did it whole-heartedly. Therefore, too, what she did was very precious in the sight of the Lord. See John 12:3-8. This passage of Scripture says very significantly: "The house was filled with the odor of the ointment."

Truly such is the case. A steady stream of blessing issues from the Mary-souls to those who come in contact with them. Not only from what they say and do, but from their whole personality. There is something holy, something of the eternal, about them. We notice in them that touch of the divine which is the real essence of holiness.

Jesus once said, "He that believeth on me, as the Scripture hath said, from within him shall flow rivers of living water" (John 7:38).

This is true of the Mary-souls.

"Mary hath chosen the good part, *which shall not be* taken away from her."

Have you chosen this good part, my dear reader?

Or are you the possessor of those things only which some day shall be taken away from you?

You are perhaps fortunate enough to own a house and home.

Naturally you love your home and take care of it as well and make it as cozy as you can. But some day you will have to part with it, without further notice. A casket will transport you away from 'it. And others will move in, only after an extra good housecleaning. They desire to obliterate thoroughly every trace of you.

You love the flowers in your garden and care for them lovingly and tenderly. Oftentimes they gladden your heart both by their beauty and their fragrance. But some day they will render you their last service: they will deck your casket. And then wither upon your grave.

You have money. And you love your money, whether you have much or little. But some day it, too, will be taken from you. Others will divide it among themselves. Your bank account will be transferred to other names.

Your abilities are in a special sense your own. And perhaps you have great ability, both physical and mental. But some day it, too, will be gone. You will not even be able to lift your hand to brush a fly from your face.

Perhaps you are a clear thinker and have a keen intellect. But some day you will lose your consciousness also and thereby the use of your faculties.

You have loved ones, who love you and who are kind to you. And you are grateful for their love.

But some day these tender ties, too, will be severed. Your loved ones will be standing by your bedside, wiping the perspiration of death from your brow and the tears from their own eyes. Through death's portal you must pass alone.

Your body, too, you will have to surrender. Today it may be sound and strong. But before you die it may become a heavy burden to you, giving you pain night and day. And when death has finally done its work, they will have to hurry and bury your body in the ground, six feet beneath the sod.

Then it is well to have the good part, which shall not be taken from us.

Everybody appreciates this, too. And therefore they desire to *die* as Christians. But, strangely enough, most of them do not desire to *live* as Christians.

"If thou hadst known in this day, even thou, the things which belong unto thy peace," Jesus said.

And He it was also who said, "One thing is needful."

When the Blind See

"What wilt thou that I shall do unto thee?"
—Mark 10:51.

JESUS spoke these words to a man by the name of Bartimaeus. This man was blind, and in those days it was very much of a foregone conclusion that he would have to beg for his livelihood. They had placed him out at the cross-roads where there was heavy traffic in those days, and no doubt many of the passers-by gave him an alms now and then. I can well imagine that while some of them stood there and picked out a coin to give to him that they spoke words similar to these:

"You, who are blind, you ought to try to get up north to Galilee where there is a remarkable man by the name of Jesus, who is supposed to hail from Nazareth. They say that He heals both rich and poor, and without charging anything. They say He heals anybody, the blind, the deaf, the lame, and the leprous, in fact, they even say that He has raised a man from the dead! Many believe that He is the Messiah."

Naturally Bartimaeus would have liked to have gone up into Galilee to see this remarkable man.

But how was he to get there, he, a blind man, who had all he could do to find his way from town to the cross-roads?

Well can we understand that Bartimaeus sat there in darkness day after day hoping that the kind man from

Nazareth would come that way at least once, in order that he might ask Him to cure him of his blindness.

And one day it really did come to pass.

He heard a noise down the road. And since he could see nothing, he asked, as usual, what it was. To which some one who stood nearby replied, "It is Jesus of Nazareth."

Bartimaeus' great opportunity had come!

He could not see any one, of course; and therefore he cried out as loudly as possible, "Jesus, thou son of David, have mercy on me."

But they all told him to hold his peace.

It was a great festive throng from Galilee. They would not go through Samaria, and for that reason they had crossed the Jordan to the north and kept to the east side of the river all the way down, and re-crossed again at Jericho.

They were going to Jerusalem to the Passover Feast, and Jesus was in their midst. He was perhaps going to the capitol city to the great feast and have Himself proclaimed as the Messiah, some thought. It was a thrilling, a festive scene.

They could not, therefore, allow a ragged beggar to delay or interfere with the festive procession. "And many rebuked him, that he should hold his peace," Mark says.

However, Bartimaeus had only this one chance, and therefore he cried out louder than the first time: "Thou son of David, have mercy on me!"

But this time Bartimaeus would not have had to cry as loudly as he did, because Jesus had already come so close that He could hear that something was wrong. And when He learned that it was a blind beggar who was calling to Him, He told them forthwith to lead the man to Him!

No doubt the kind words and the gentle voice of Jesus
had already been a blessing to the blind man—he was not
particularly accustomed to such friendliness.

He became so happy that "he, casting away his gar-
ment, sprang up, and came to Jesus," even though he was
blind.

"What wilt thou that I should do unto thee?"

Bartimaeus was certainly in no doubt about that, and
answered in tense expectation:

"Rabboni, that I may receive my sight!"

"Receive thy sight!" said Jesus.

And Bartimaeus saw.

The first one he saw was Jesus.

Is it strange that we are told that he began to glorify
God then and there as he followed Him in the way?

And his example spread. Luke relates that when the
pilgrims on the way to the feast heard Bartimaeus thank
and praise God, they too, gave praise unto the Lord.

Indeed, songs of praise arise in every way where Jesus
does His mighty works. Also in our day. Many old,
withered Christians are refreshed and become like children again when they see the Lord open the eyes of the
blind and when they hear the shouts of praise of the
newly converted.

＊

I am especially fond of this story.

We have many wonderful stories about Jesus in the
Bible. It is not easy to say which we prize most highly.

I, however, am particularly in love with this one. It
gives me a picture of my Savior which does my heart a
great deal of good.

Here I see Him in all His regal greatness and goodness.

Think of it: He is so great that He can go about in the
ways of earth and say to those whom He meets, "What
wilt thou that I shall do unto thee?" And when we poor

suppliants have presented our pleas, He can fulfil them, no matter what we ask of Him.

His regal goodness is so great that He does not turn away from any one who in his need turns to Him.

The most hypocritical liar, the biggest scoundrel, the most licentious whoremonger, the most painted woman of the street, the worst perjurer, the boldest robber and murderer—as soon as He hears a sincere prayer from any of them, He turns aside to them and asks, "What wilt thou that I shall do unto thee?"

When we read the gospels, we note that Jesus turned first to those who were in distress. His eye searched out the suffering.

And if this book should fall into the hands of some one who is especially heavy laden, then I would ask such a one to listen in particular to these words: Jesus turns first of all to the suppliants of earth.

Perhaps you have become a spiritual beggar. You know of no way out. Life has become so burdensome to you that you do not know how you can carry the load any longer. I have some wonderful, good news for you. Jesus is standing before you and asking, "What wilt thou that I shall do unto thee?"

As long as you have not taken your troubles to Jesus, you should not say that you do not know what to do.

Why do you not go to this mighty friend of yours?

Do you know yourself why you do not seek the help of Him who died for you?

Are you afraid to let Him help you?

Are you afraid that He will help you more than you desire?

Perhaps you are afraid that He will restore your spiritual sight?

There are many who would rather continue in their blindness than to have their spiritual sight restored. To be reconciled to God and to break with their former manner of life they look upon as the worst misfortune that could ever befall them.

Oh, how full the world is of *blind* people!

*

What a joy it is to be a Christian!

Think of having a friend who can help us in our every need, who stands before us each day and asks, "What wilt thou that I shall do unto thee?"

Who awakens us every morning with this question. And who gives us permission to begin the day by telling Him what we will need most during the day.

It seems to me that we who have such a friend should cease whining and complaining. Instead, we should sing praises unto God, as Bartimaeus and the pilgrims on the way to the feast did.

We are journeying onward to a greater feast than the Passover which they were to celebrate in Jerusalem. We are on the way to the feast eternal in the heavenly Jerusalem. And Jesus is in our midst. And He performs mighty acts now as then.

Let us praise His name in such a way that heaven and earth will know that He has some very grateful and happy friends.

Some of the friends of Jesus do not believe that He does wonders any more. They do not doubt that He did wonders 1900 years ago. But they do not think that He does them now.

When preaching on the miracles of Jesus, which, by the way, occur in nearly every Sunday's Gospel lesson, the miracles are usually—with remarkable ingenuity— dealt with in a *spiritual* way only, even though the text speaks as clearly as daylight about a *physical* miracle.

As a result, many a friend of Jesus sits in his pew and sighs in deep physical, temporal distress, and thinks in his own quiet mind: "Oh, that I had lived in the time of Jesus! Then I could have put on my best clothes and set out upon a journey to where Jesus was; and persuaded Him to come along with me to my home, where there is so much sickness and misery."

My suffering friend!

Jesus has not ceased to perform miracles. He performs them now as before.

He would *gladly* do wonders for you too.

Have you not read in the gospels about the woman whom He asked to be brought to Him in the synagogue? And how He healed her on the Sabbath before the very eyes of the Pharisees, although He knew that they would object? They *said,* too, that He should have waited until the Sabbath was passed.

But to this Jesus replied, "And ought not this woman, being a daughter of Abraham, whom Satan had bound, lo, these eighteen years, to have been loosed from this bond on the day of the Sabbath?"

Indeed, Jesus would gladly have employed His wonder-working powers in behalf of His suffering fellowmen, but He was often prevented from doing so by their unbelief. Every now and then we read that Jesus could do no mighty works in that place because of their unbelief. We are also told that He marvelled at their unbelief.

Today, too, Jesus marvels at our unbelief. He waits for us to ask Him to perform miracles.

If you are in distress now, if you yourself are sick, or one of your dear ones, then ask Jesus to do wonders for you. Tell Him how much you need His supernatural intervention. Tell Him how happy you would be, not only to receive His help, but most of all to have Him answer your prayers openly, and to see one of His miracles.

And remember when you pray for this that Jesus is glad to do wonders, to make use of His powers on behalf of His friends.

But, having said this much, I also feel the desire to say a little more.

You and I may freely *ask* the Lord to perform miracles, any kind of miracle. But we must never *demand* miracles, or command Him to perform wonders.

He will not suffer that. He will not on the whole allow us to command Him. He is God, and there is none besides Him.

Therefore we ought to pray for miracles in a childlike and humble way, telling God how much we need to have Him work wonders and how much we would like to have Him perform such. We can put it simply and directly, like this: "If it will glorify Thy name, then perform this miracle of healing in our home. But if it will *not* glorify Thy name, then do not do it. Let us rather be sick. But in that event Thou must in Thy grace and mercy perform another miracle, namely, that of giving us strength to glorify Thy name through sickness and tribulation."

And let us also try to remember that a miracle of *this* kind is no less a miracle than sudden physical healing.

*

I do not know if you have ever stopped to ponder the fact that Jesus asked the blind man what he wanted. Might not Jesus have known this without asking?

You perhaps expect me to give you a profound answer to this question, like certain Bible teachers who have more imagination than Bible knowledge.

But I cannot do that. In fact I have no answer at all.

But though I do not understand why Jesus asked the blind man what he wanted, there is one thing I do understand, and which is very closely related to it.

I can understand why Jesus must ask His friends, "What do you want?"

I know a man who has been on his knees before the Lord hundreds of times. And if I, after having said, Amen, had remained there long enough to give the Lord time to ask me: "But what do you want?" I would have had to answer: "Thanks, there wasn't anything I wanted. I only wanted to pray!"

Jesus often meets such friends of His in the secret places of prayer. They do not have a good conscience unless they have prayed a little. But there is really nothing they *desire* when they pray.

This grieves the Lord Jesus. He sees, of course, that we need many things. He knows, moreover, that His heaven is full of those very gifts which would transform us from stunted, starved, and emaciated Christians to sound, strong, happy, crusading Christians. Then you can realize why He feels like asking, "What *wilt* thou? Is there anything you *want* of me?"

You perhaps remember well the time in your Christian life when you knew what you wanted when you went into your secret chamber to pray.

Your need, the distress which you felt because of sin, constrained you to pray. When you had grieved your Savior, you could not find peace until you had slipped away for a moment from the noise and bustle and from your work and quietly told your Savior everything.

Those were times when you wept in the secret chamber. But not only tears of sorrow. O how happy you were when you became reconciled again, and everything was right once more between you and your Lord. He had spoken to you the blessed words, "Be of good cheer, thy sins are forgiven."

*

Bartimaeus knew what he wanted.

He wanted to see.

We human beings differ somewhat, but not as much as we have, for some time, been thinking. And if we were to tell the Savior what we wanted Him to do for us now, very likely our desires would vary somewhat.

But likely some of us would pray about like Bartimaeus did: "Lord, that I may receive my *sight!*"

You have perhaps noticed for some time that there is something wrong with your inner vision. You do not see so well any longer as you did before.

You could see things better before when you read your Bible.

Do you remember what you *saw* when you read the Bible with the eye of simple and childlike faith? Even the most insignificant things took on a large meaning and were a source of edification to you, because you saw God in them. You read and gave thanks to Him.

Especially did you look forward to Sunday. You had more time to read then. On that day you would sit quietly for hours and read chapter after chapter. And, verily, you beheld His glory!

Can you remember how happy you were when reading the Bible? You perhaps carried a pocket Testament with you. Women, having no pockets, would carry the Testament in their purse. At home you laid your Testament on a shelf or a table nearby, so you could easily reach for it in the midst of your work.

And when you took a moment's rest, you reached for the Testament. You had perhaps entered into an agreement with God and yourself, that wherever your right thumb was when you opened the book, you would read.

You read that little verse. And you *saw!* Oh, the things that God sometimes let you see in that moment!

Do you see that well now when you read your Bible?

Or do you not see anything any more? Has reading the
Bible become a burden to you, a sort of compromise
with your conscience? You read a portion merely for the
sake of having read, do you not!

You could see better before also in matters pertaining
to your daily life.

Do you remember how strict you were with yourself
in your home life? Not only in regard to what you did
and said, but also what you thought. Do you remember
how terribly it hurt you when you had been unkind to one
of your dear ones and had grieved your Savior?

Do you see that well now? Are you as strict with
yourself now as you were formerly?

You could see better before also when looking at your
fellow men.

It is indeed touching to see new converts as they
begin to look upon their fellow beings in a new light.
They begin to look upon them with the eye of Jesus.
They see that they are immortal souls for whom Jesus
has shed His life-blood.

That is why it is so terrible to see them thoughtlessly
despise the Savior and trample His blood under foot.

As for you, you could not endure to see it without
speaking to them about their immortal souls. To begin
with they were perhaps kind and courteous, and listened
to you. But afterwards they became impatient and said to
you, "Now you must keep still a while! You make life
impossible for us with all your preaching!"

Soon you yourself began to feel that way. You, too,
felt that you had better be quiet, and not tire them out
with your admonitions.

You tried to keep still.

But do you remember that as you walked among them
and kept silence tears rolled down your cheeks?

Then it was that you could *see* well.

Do you see any of that now when you look upon your fellow men?

Or has your sight been impaired to such an extent that you do not see immortal souls any more when you see men?

There are many Christians who no longer see the soul-needs of men. They no longer see that the unconverted people they are associating with from day to day are souls which should be *won* for God, and which God would have won *through them*.

Oh, the many believers who no longer have any burden upon their hearts for the sheep which have been lost from the fold.

And still there are people who ask why we do not have more spiritual awakenings!

This is not strange to me. On the contrary, it is an incomprehensible miracle to me that God can send us a spiritual awakening at all when there are so many of us believers who are not burdened by the soul-needs of men.

❋

What *wilt* thou now?

Would you be healed? Would you have your sight restored?

Think a while; do not answer too quickly. The question before us is a serious one. Consider well whether you really desire to be healed.

Of course I desire to be healed, you say. Is there a Christian believer anywhere who, when shown his spiritual ailment, does not desire to be healed?

Unfortunately, there are many such.

They began well.

God succeeded in overpowering their old, selfish egos, and they surrendered themselves unreservedly to Him; and He filled their hearts with the love of Christ.

But a change took place during a time of spiritual weakening, perhaps as a result of spiritual undernourishment. They began to listen to the tempter's voice: "Spare thyself."

Immediately they discovered a number of valid reasons for according themselves a little more consideration. And then, well, then they drifted slowly but certainly into *sacrifice-less* Christianity, that type which first of all looks to its own comfort, pleasure, and advantage.

By so doing these people provided themselves with an easy, comfortable type of Christianity, a type which neither Old Adam, nor the world, nor the devil has anything against.

Nor do they by any means have any idea of parting with this form of Christianity.

They look upon it almost as their personal gift of grace. With their experience in life, their knowledge of human nature, their cleverness and wisdom they have been able to plan their Christian life in such a practical and sensible way that they do not run into all sorts of conflicts and difficulties as they did to begin with!

No; they have no desire to be healed!

They do not care to have their sight restored. They do not desire a keener vision than they already have; that would make life too strenuous and uncomfortable.

*

What is it that causes the impairment of our spiritual vision? *Sin.* That is what attacks our spiritual eyes.

There is this to be noted, however, that it is not sin itself which attacks the optical nerves of our spiritual life. Not even the coarsest sin can destroy our spiritual vision if it is confessed before God immediately and with a sincerity which knows no consideration of any kind.

But, on the other hand, the smallest sin is sufficient to weaken and, at last, destroy our vision if it is not acknowledged as sin before God, but is excused, defended, or bedecked

Here we touch upon a point which is of decisive importance, decisive because it not only determines whether we are to go forward or backward in sanctification, but also whether we are to be eternally saved or not. For the falling away in the lives of believers *begins* without any doubt at this point. Unconfessed sin impairs our spiritual vision until total blindness at last results. "If therefore the light that is in thee be darkness, how great is the darkness!" (Matthew 6:23).

Permit me to mention two things which are especially dangerous to the believer. Perhaps they are more dangerous than anything else to the majority of Christians, even though we must reckon with some individual differences.

The first thing I would mention is *money*.

What about your finances?

I am not asking you whether you have little or much money. What I would like to know is, who is lord, you or your money?

I do not know how things are with you now. But if God has ever converted your heart, I know that you know of a time in your life when God made you lord over your means.

You perhaps remember that time very well. You lived in intimate co-partnership with God, and consulted Him in all your financial affairs, when you bought and sold, as well as when you were planning to give to the needy or to the work of the Lord.

What an intimate and confidential relationship there was between you and God!

But there was an Old Adam in you, too. He is always a devoted servant of mammon. What he wants to do with money first and foremost is to *have his way* with it.

He always thinks that God is impractical when it comes to money matters, in fact, that God is uneconomical!

As a result the temptation came to you to take your financial affairs into your own hands. And you yielded to the temptation. You thought that by so doing you would be putting your financial affairs upon a better basis. Whereupon you proceeded to take charge of your own finances.

By so doing you did not, of course, intend to give up Christianity; you continued to read the Bible and pray as before.

But you noticed a change, nevertheless. It seemed as though it was impossible to get in touch with God again. Every time you started to pray it seemed as though you could not think of anything else but your self-managed financial affairs.

It was the Spirit of God who was mercifully trying to make you restless, and who with this in mind kept crying to you while you prayed: "Money! Money! Money!"

The same story repeated itself when you read the Bible. You came across something about money and the love of money continually. It seemed to you as though the Bible spoke of nothing else but money.

And when you went to church or to meetings it seemed as though the preachers had all entered into an agreement to speak about nothing else but money.

Just like when you have hurt your finger. You seem to strike the injured member all the time and never the uninjured ones. Of course, you strike them too; but you do not feel it. Whenever you strike your aching finger you feel it, simply because it is sensitive.

You did not notice before how often you read and heard about the love of money. Now you notice it, because now you have a deep, open sore in your conscience on this very point.

But perhaps love of mammon is not your bosom sin?
May I then ask you another question:
"How about your home life?"
"Do you get along well? Do you love each other? Are you cordial toward one another?"
Especially do these questions have a message to us married folk.
Do you live in a loving, intimate, forgiving relationship with each other?
You remember a time at least when you were happy and cordial toward each other. Never can you forget the deep, peaceful joy which was yours at that time.
You read the Bible together; you knelt together; you prayed together; you sang together; you conversed together about everything in heaven and on earth. You experienced the wonderful joys of a Christian home, without having either riches or costly furniture! Not a place on earth is so close to paradise lost as the Christian home.
But none of us are perfect.
We all have some sharp corners; and when we live together day by day as married folk do, it often happens that those corners of ours rub against each other.
One day your wife, or your husband, let fall a few sharp words. You answered just a little more sharply. And before either one of you realized it you were having a scene which was terrible indeed.
After the words had been spoken, the Spirit of God came and said to you, "Ask for forgiveness!"
"Yes," you replied, "I could do that, too; but this time at least it was not I who started it."
"That is true enough," said the Spirit, "but you were enough at fault, too, to ask for forgiveness."
And you did. And well do you remember how happy you were. It *is* good to humble one's self. And we all

feel that it is exceedingly humiliating to ask for forgiveness.

But this happened again and again. Finally you began to grow weary.

You said to yourself, "This time somebody else can ask for forgiveness." You became callous. And since you were perhaps the stronger-willed one in your home, it was finally you who decided where the cupboard was to stand.

But it brought you no happiness.

After that things were closed against you, not only upwards, toward God, but also between the two of you, husband and wife. No cordiality. No more praying together. No more singing together. No more conversation about the things of God. At most, routine family worship, which you disposed of as briefly as possible.

Thus many Christian homes have been plunged into ruin!

Neither of the two give up fearing God. But they no longer share these things with each other. From now on they live their Christian lives by themselves. The one at his office work, the other at her home duties; the one in the barn, the other in the pantry.

*

Would you be healed?

Now perhaps you understand better why I asked you to be cautious and to weigh the matter carefully before answering. Now you see what it involves to be healed.

If your spiritual sight is restored to you, you cannot continue to live the life you are now living. You will have to submit to the convicting work of the Spirit of God. He has said all along that you were *miserly* and a lover of filthy lucre, but you have continued to defend yourself by saying that you were only *economical*. If you now admit that He is right, you will have to give up managing your financial affairs selfishly, and let the Lord have His way with you.

Will you do that? Do you dare to do that?

You who have wronged your wife or your husband, you cannot continue thus if your sight is restored to you and you see the grave injustice which you have done. You will have to humble yourself before the one you have wronged and say, "Will you forgive me? It is I who am to blame that we are so unhappy in our home."

Will you do that? Are you able to do that?

There are many unhappy souls in the various Christian circles, souls without peace, joy, or strength, souls who are bound hand and foot by the sins which they will not seek to overcome and which they consequently will not confess. Sins which the Spirit of God calls to their remembrance, but which they will not confess as sin, but rather seek to excuse and defend.

Many of these unhappy souls, too, long earnestly for release from their bondage.

They remember the time when they had peace with God in a good conscience. Their relationships with God were in the clear and in the open; they could look Him in the eye, so to speak, not because they were sinless, but because they did not try to conceal anything, and because it was their heart's desire to speak with God about everything.

They were happy then because they were not afraid of the Spirit of God or of the truth which He spoke. On the contrary, to know that the Spirit was telling them the full truth was precisely what made them feel happy and secure.

As I have said before, there are many souls with their backs firmly fettered to the wall, so to speak, who earnestly long to be set free.

But nothing more comes of it except longing. They cannot effect their own release. They are as if paralyzed. They have been rendered impotent by their own sins.

It is too hard for them to humble themselves. Every time they are about to decide to break with their sins, they shrink back.

It is to such that Jesus directs these wonderful words, "What wilt thou that I shall do unto thee?"

You have been thinking all along of what *you* should do. And as a result there has been no change in your life. You cannot in your own strength do what in this case must be done.

Listen now to what Jesus says: "What wilt thou that *I shall do unto thee?* Here is the way out. Jesus will do for you what you have not been able to do for yourself. He proclaims liberty to the captive and opens the prison to them that are bound, He says.

All you need to do is to tell Him your troubles. But you must tell Him *all*. Tell Him not only that you have sinned, but also that you have tried to evade the truth, that you have tried to make yourself believe that your wrongdoings were not sinful. Tell Him how bound and fettered you are, and that you are unable to extricate yourself.

He will perform a miracle and save you.

How He will do it is not so easy to say. We cannot always comprehend His wondrous ways. The important thing, however, is that the miracle actually does take place in our lives.

I think, however, that His way of healing you will be a good deal like the way He healed Bartimaeus. His *sight* was restored, and he beheld *Jesus*.

He will save you, too, by enabling you in a miraculous way to *see Jesus*.

It is a long time now since you have seen Him. You

have not seen Him since the unfortunate occurrence which I have described took place in your inner life.

In fact, in the last analysis, your real misfortune has been that you have not seen Jesus during all this time. You have undoubtedly desired to see Him, and perhaps tried also. But without result.

What was the reason for this?

Your unconfessed sins, which rose up against you and shielded the Cross from your eyes.

Your inner eye sought the Cross as before. But no matter which way you turned, you could not see the Cross.

You read the old, well known promises, but no; no consolation!

You listened to the same preachers, but went away with the same restlessness and emptiness of soul.

You asked the Spirit of God to help you. But He gave you no peace. He could not, as a matter of fact. It would have meant that you would have been lost if He had given you peace in the condition in which you were.

No, in order to save you He had to make your wicked and rebellious heart restless and anxious. He has succeeded in doing *this very thing.* He has made you so restless that you cannot persevere in your sinful relationship toward Him any longer. You are now willing to *confess* your sins.

Now you can *see Jesus* again.

Your view of the Cross is unobstructed. As soon as we confess the sins which we formerly excused and defended, that which has hidden the Cross from our eyes falls away.

The Spirit of God can now declare Christ unto you again. He can now explain the Cross to you once more. He can now point to the Lamb of God, who has taken away all your sins, also those sins which you have made doubly sinful by your deceitfulness and your secret defense of them.

He brings to your remembrance the old promises, which now sound new and fresh to your ears. God Himself speaks gently to your bruised and fearful heart. Now you no longer have to arrogate unto yourself some kind of faith or *steal* grace. He showers His goodness upon you.

You feel as ashamed as the prodigal son was when his father received him, gave him the best robe, put shoes on his feet and a ring on his finger, and made a feast for him.

Verily, there is nothing so unfathomable as the grace of God!

And of grace again nothing is so unfathomable as grace *experienced!*

Grace not only gives you peace, joy, and assurance that your sins are forgiven.

It gives you *power* also.

It gives you strength to go to your husband or wife and ask for forgiveness; it gives you power to cease being miserly.

You cannot understand how it is, but now you are willing to do these things of your own accord. That is because you have seen Jesus. You now experience the truth of the deep and mysterious words: "It is God who worketh in you both to will and to work, for His good pleasure" (Philippians 2:13).

New power comes into your withered Christian life at every point. A *willing* spirit moves into your life again. And the resulting change can hardly be adequately described.

How unwilling, contrary, and perverse you had been throughout this whole unhappy period! You wanted to have a part in Christian life and in Christian work, in fact it was a matter of much concern to you to be considered as good a Christian as you had ever been.

But how often were you not tired of all that they expected of you. They looked to you to sacrifice both time and energy and interest and money. And there were new demands all the time! Oftentimes you became real angry with the leaders, who, it appeared to you, did nothing else but devise new ways of raising money.

Every time you heard someone complain about too many drives for raising money and too many Christian organizations in the field, you felt inwardly relieved, and said to yourself that there were at least some sensible people left in the world!

But note the difference now, since a willing spirit has been created in your heart again. Now you desire to do these things. No one needs to drive you to do them. You want to work and sacrifice. If there is anything that bothers you now it is the thought that you and all the rest do too little for the Lord and for the salvation of souls.

You have begun to *see*. You see souls and their needs. You suffer with them and pray for them. You are in the work with all your heart, and you are glad to take part in it as much as you possibly can. You thank the Lord for every heart which is willing to sacrifice and for every one who lends a hand in the work of the vineyard.

Happily, you have been cured of the spirit of bitter criticism which formerly cast its shadows into your soul and upon your work.

Closing Words

IT was in the midst of a great spiritual awakening in Galilee. People were streaming in from all sides and were crowding each other so much that they were trampling upon each other, the gospel writer says. Jesus therefore told the people to sit down on the hillside which sloped gently towards the sea. He Himself entered into a boat, from which He addressed them. Mark 4.

When evening came, He proposed to His friends that they cross over to the east side of the lake and seek rest, which both He and His disciples were in need of at the close of the day's work.

And as soon as they had said good-bye to the last ones who wanted to speak with Him, they started out.

Now, Jesus was tired and therefore lay in the stern of the boat asleep. They even had a little cushion along for Him. As for the disciples, He let them take the oars. They were not tired, as was the case with Him; the reason He had suggested that they make the trip with Him was to get them away from the multitude for a while.

Jesus Himself, however, was so tired that He went to sleep at once.

The disciples rowed. No doubt they also conversed about many things on the way over. To them it had been indeed a day replete with experiences.

So taken up were they in their conversation that they did not even notice the approaching storm. Suddenly a fearful squall broke; a great wave struck them, and water poured into the boat until it was about to sink.

And Jesus slept on.

But they cried to Him and awoke Him. Not exactly in a pleasant tone of voice either. "Teacher, carest Thou not that we perish?" they shrieked.

Whereupon He raised Himself up in the boat and said a few words to the elements in a language which they understood. At once the wind ceased, and there was a great calm.

This done, He turned to His friends and said, "Were you actually afraid? How could you think that the boat could go under as long as I was in it?"

They did not become ashamed, however; they became something else which was even better. They became exceedingly *fearful* of Him, whom even the wind and the sea obeyed.

The boat trip had indeed been an eventful one to all of them.

However, it was only six-seven miles across; and they were soon over.

*

But it was not easy for Jesus to get any rest. Wherever He went, some one who was in need cried to Him for help.

They had scarcely reached the other side before two insane men, possessed with demons, came rushing down the grassy incline to meet Him. They shrieked and yelled fiercely. It is not very likely that any of the disciples wanted to be the first to go ashore. Most likely Jesus had to take the lead. But He was not afraid. He stepped out of the boat, and commanded the unclean spirits to depart from the two unfortunates who stood before Him.

But the spirits entreated Him for permission to enter

into a large herd of swine, about two thousand in number, which was feeding on the fine mountain pasturage.

And, strangely enough, Jesus gave them the permission they sought. But when they had entered into the swine, the latter became so violent that they rushed down the steep into the lake and were drowned.

The account does not explain why Jesus gave them this permission. And I must confess that I do not understand why He did it either. But, remarkably enough, I am just as happy for that.

*

Before I was not that way.

I thought that I had to understand and be able to interpret everything that Jesus said and did, as many Bible teachers still think. This is very unfortunate, and leads to some of the strangest and most unbelievable "interpretations."

All of us are born with the desire to comprehend God. Many go so far that they even *demand* the right to be able to comprehend Him. They have no use for a God whom they cannot comprehend.

At one time in my life I was in complete accord with this idea.

And since the God of the Bible cannot be comprehended fully, I joined the ranks of those theologians who thought that the greatest problem of the day was to provide humanity with another god, a god that could be understood perfectly.

So we went to work to make a god.

The Germans were especially gifted along this line. They took the lead and soon were teaching nearly all of the theologians of Europe what the god of the modern man should be like.

He must not be fashioned out of stone or wood, as people thought in times past.

By no means; he must be a *spiritual* concept of the divine, which, consequently, made it much more difficult. Nor was there always unanimity regarding details. In one respect, however, they were fully agreed: the god of the modern man had to be *comprehensible*.

And after we had formed our spiritual concept of God, we fell down and worshipped it.

But I remember well from that time in my life that I really had very little use for this god. Of course, he was comprehensible enough—we had made him ourselves. But, remarkably enough, no particularly intimate relationships between us and this god were developed. I had to overcome myself to the very limit in order to accord him the modest modicum of worship which we in our wisdom deemed sufficient.

But then the most remarkable thing in my life happened. I really began to have need of God, for the living God. In a way that I to this day cannot explain, my sin became so unbearable that I could not live without being saved from its guilt and power.

But then the remarkable thing also happened that I no longer could get along with a god that I could understand perfectly. I had to seek the God whose ways are past finding out. I had to go to the God who gave His life as a propitiation for my sins, to Him who raised up the Cross, the enigma of offense, in the world.

The Cross, the most incomprehensible thing of all in connection with the God of the Bible, became the dearest and most indispensable of all to my broken and contrite heart.

Moreover, since that day neither God nor the Cross have become any more comprehensible to me. But that in no wise hinders me from believing in Him and loving Him.

The more I learn to know God, the more I understand that God is and must be incomprehensible. The irrational, the super-rational, element in God no longer offends my reason. It seems clear to me that God must be a few degrees above my little understanding. That no doubt belongs to Him as God. Only to *create* the world God had to be able to do something that I not only could not *do*, but could not even *understand*.

The longer I live, the more I thank God that I cannot fully comprehend Him. For if He were no greater than my power to comprehend Him, He certainly would not be able to govern this world, not to speak of saving it.

Many people think that it is impossible to trust in a God whom they cannot fully understand.

Strange what theorists and doctrinaires can say and write!

What we know about our own children is sufficient to teach us that confidence or trust is not dependent upon ability to comprehend fully the one in whom we place our trust.

Children ask about everything, possible and impossible. All of which is right and proper, because that is the way their little minds arrive at consciousness and self-expression. But it cannot be denied nevertheless that they ask about things to which we can give them no answer, because they are too young as yet to understand.

As a rule boys ask the most questions. When one of my boys asks me about such things, I say to him: "I cannot tell you that now, my boy; but wait until you grow older; then I will explain the whole thing to you."

What do you think he does when I answer him in that way?

Do you think he goes and sits down in a chair and cries and says, "It is impossible to be in a home where you have a father who does not answer all the questions you ask him"?

No, he does not. He runs right out and plays with the other children as before,—and no doubt forgets to close the door as he goes.

Do you not see that the little lad retains his childlike confidence in me as he has always done, even though I do not explain to him everything that he asks about?

Yes, indeed, it is possible to trust God even if we ask Him about things to which He cannot give us an answer until we see Him in His heavenly glory!

As far as that is concerned, I am not certain that He will explain everything to us there either. It is extremely likely that God's ways are so far past finding out that we will never understand Him perfectly. On the other hand, He has promised us that we shall *behold* Him. And when we have done that, I think we shall be forever cured of the idea of comprehending God. Then I think we will really have seen how incomprehensibly great He is.

*

Well, this was a long digression.

Let us turn back to the swine. They drowned. And those who had fed them fled into the city and related the stirring incident. Before long the whole town was at the scene of destruction to see and to hear what had happened.

And there stood Jesus.

If not in words, then in deeds He now asked the great multitude, "What will ye that I should do unto you?"

Do you remember, dear reader, what they answered?

Jesus was visiting them this one time. He had shown them in a convincing way what He could do. And He had manifested to them His grace and mercy by ministering to the two men for whom nobody thought anything could be done.

But their united plea was that Jesus would *depart from their borders to another place!*

That was the only prayer they had to offer to Jesus. And they were all in one accord about it, too.

If it were not for the fact that we are so accustomed to hearing and reading this, it would send cold shivers down our spines when we read that these people had nothing else to ask of Jesus this one time that He was visiting them.

But there is something much worse than this, and that is that these people are not the only ones who have asked Jesus to depart from them and go somewhere else.

It has been done during all these hundreds of years and in all lands.

Whole families, whole neighborhoods, have prayed this prayer with one accord when Jesus came into their midst of His own volition. He spoke mildly but seriously to the souls of men, and did His mighty works in their midst. They could not doubt but that it was Jesus who was in their midst.

And by his own mighty deeds He asked them the fateful question, "What will ye that I should do unto you?"

My dear reader!

What did you answer?

Have you, too, prayed Jesus that you might be spared from religious unrest and the upbraidings of conscience? Have you, too, asked Him to permit you to sin in peace?

Yes, you have done that very thing, you say, not only once but many times.

I do not doubt that. That is what most people do when Jesus seeks to gain an entrance into their lives.

But listen, Jesus is here again, knocking at your heart's door.

You cannot drive Him away by rejecting and despising

Him. You can not exhaust His love by your rebelliousness.

"Is that true?" some one says.

"Then I can never be lost! Then there is no hell! That
is just what I have thought in my own mind! If God is
as loving as the preachers say He is, He certainly cannot
have the heart to cast any one into hell!"

Very well; others before you have undoubtedly thought
likewise.

But you have forgotten one important thing. Christ's
love is perfect love. He left heaven for our sakes. He
gave Himself in death to save us. And it is *He* who says
that there is an everlasting hell. And He says, furthermore, that the love of God cannot alter *that* fact.

Christ says that, since He has died for sin, there is now
no need of anyone going to hell, because He can save
them. But He also says that they who *reject* His salvation
cannot avoid hell. Not even *He* can prevent such souls
from landing in everlasting torment.

They do not go to hell because He has ceased to love
them and have compassion on them, but because they have
brought themselves into a spiritual condition in which
even almighty God is helpless and has no means by which
to save them.

How does this take place?

This is a very quiet and simple process. It is just
what you and many others have done every time that
Jesus has knocked at your heart's door and offered to
save you. You have rejected Him.

No one can set at nought the laws which govern
soul-life.

Every one who time after time experiences a strong
inner conviction, but *will* not follow it, loses successively
the faculty of becoming convinced. And Jesus has only
one way of saving men, and that is by *convincing* them.

That man is therefore hopelessly lost who by repeatedly despising and opposing the gracious call of God unto salvation has wasted and destroyed his soul's capacity for being convinced.

And if you think that God sits up there in His heaven and looks down in malicious glee upon those who despise Him, you are thoroughly mistaken.

If you would like to know how He feels when He sees them in all the hopelessness of their lost condition, then read the little account in Luke 19:41-44:

Jesus draws nigh and sees the city which has rejected all His proffers of salvation and is therefore ripe for the judgment which must come. And with prophetic vision Jesus also sees the judgment which after a few years will be visited upon the rebellious city.

And He weeps.

Such is God. That is what love does when it has exhausted every means of saving the loved one.

God's saving love must mean to all of us one of two things, either eternal *salvation* or eternal *damnation*.

Many speak with much feeling about the seriousness of *death*. Which is true. Death is a serious matter to all of us.

But it is a constant source of wonder to me that there are so many who do not see the seriousness of *life*. There is unquestionably a greater risk connected with life than with death.

But we have a Savior who frees us from all the dangers connected with both life and death. By forgiving us the sins of life, He removes from us the sting of death.